A SYMPHONY OF LIFE

RAJAT CHANDRA SARMAH

BookLeaf Publishing
India | USA | UK

Presentation by *BookLeaf Publishing*

Web: www.bookleafpub.com

E-mail: info@bookleafpub.com

ISBN: 9789363314269

First edition 2024

To

My dear sons

Pratik and Prantik

with love

Papa

ACKNOWLEDGEMENT

I sincerely acknowledge the opportunity being given by the Bookleaf Publication for the wonderful programme of the writing challenge on poetry for 21 days and subsequent publication. It helped a newcomer to publish his work and come to the readers for their reactions. This was a great opportunity.

I also acknowledge my family and friends for their constant encouragement to take up the challenge and complete it successfully.

I always feel it is the wish of the Almighty; without the blessing of the Almighty, nothing can move forward. I hope I will always get the blessing in all my future endeavours.

Rajat Chandra Sarmah

PREFACE

I was never a poet and struggled with literature during my school days. My teachers frequently advised me to give more importance to literature, even providing me with excellent books to read. Despite their efforts, I did not perform well in my final literature examinations and pursued a career in engineering instead. A few more marks in literature could have changed my life altogether, but it was not to be. Since then, I have harboured the thought that one day I would excel in literature and have my work read and acclaimed by many.

This internal drive compelled me to take up writing only after retiring from service. My first book, "A Sanguine Tale: Unfolding the Life of a Project Engineer," was widely acclaimed, earning me the title of Best Emerging Author in the Non-Fiction category at the Kolkata Literary Carnival 2024 and the Golden Book of the Year Award 2024. My second book, "A New Dawn: Adventure in the Golden Years," became an Amazon Best Seller, reaching No. 1, and my third book, "Whisper of The Diverse Tales," a collection of short stories, was published in 2024. I was also awarded the International

Tagore Award on the specialist genre of Literature in 2024 by DRDC.

Until now, I had not ventured into poetry, finding it the most challenging form of writing. However, my curiosity and determination led me to consider trying my hand at it. Around this time, I came across an advertisement from BookLeaf Publishing for the #TheWriteAngle Writing Challenge, which involved writing 21 poems in 21 days. I saw this as the perfect opportunity to step into the world of poetry, the most daunting genre for me. Embracing the challenge, I soon found words flowing to me, gaining the confidence to believe I could succeed.

I dedicated myself fully to the contest and completed writing 21 poems on various subjects. It would bring me great joy if my readers appreciated these poems and encouraged me to continue my writing journey.

Readers can connect with me via email at **rajatchandrasarmah@gmail.com** and also via my Instagram: **rajatchandrasarmah5**

PUBLISHED WORK
OF
RAJAT CHANDRA SARMAH

Sanguine tale unfolding the life of a Project Engineer (English)
(ISBN 979-8-88704-866-6
Book link: https://amzn.in/d/02xkVwdV

Award:

A) Emerging writer of the year (Non-Fiction) at Kolkata Literary Carnival 2024.

B) Golden Book Award 2024

2. CHINESE VERSION ISBN: 978939201382
Book Link: https://amzn.eu/d/eSp7r1m

3. FRENCH VERSION (A la vie d'un ingénieur CONTE de projet SANGLANT) ISBN:9789359208657

Book Link: https://a.co/d/0iPjo381

4. SPANISH VERSION (UN desarrollo de la vida de un ingeniero CUENTO de proyectos SANGRIENTO)
ISBN :9789359202426

Book Link: https://amzn.in/d/08a9mmXL

5. A NEW DAWN ADVENTURE IN THE GOLDEN YEARS
AMAZON BEST SELLER NUMBER #1
ISBN:978-93-5847-577-7

Book Link: https://amzn.in/d/0bdbOXNi

6. WHISPER OF THE DIVERSE TALES (A COLLECTION OF SHORT STORIES)
ISBN: 97893626697486

Book Link: https://amzn.in/d/09vvPKso

7. CO-AUTHOR - THOSE BROKEN WHISPERS VOLUME -I
ISBN:9789360498528

Book Link: https://amzn.in/d/03eriz4d

Under publication

Behind The Headlines (English Fiction Thriller)

TABLE OF CONTENTS

Love and Relationship

Love That Blooms

In gardens where the roses grow,
Beneath the moon's soft, silvery glow,
Our love took root, its origins slight,
A tender seed in the quiet night.

Among petals bathed in morning dew,
Where light reveals each shade of blue,
Our hearts weave in a promise true,
In colors bright and shadows too.

With every dawn, new petals rise,
Reflecting dreams in lovers' eyes,
In twilight's grace, beneath wide skies,
Our bond blooms on; it never dies.

Through spring's lush fields and summer's heat,
In autumn's gold and winter's sleet,
Our love endures each heartbeat,
A garden where our spirits meet.

In winds that carry whispers low,
In gentle rains that softly flow,
Our love expands, begins to grow,
A witness to what we know.

When storms arise with thunder's claim,
And lightning strikes without refrain,
Our bond holds firm, remains the same,
In steadfast faith through joy and pain.

As years go by and seasons change,
Our love's a landscape, vast and strange,
In endless fields, beyond the range,
Of what mere words can rearrange.

For in the soil where roses climb,
Our hearts find rhythm from time to time,
In every rhyme and every chime,
Our love, a rose, continues its prime.

Through days of sun and nights of cold,
In tales of both new and old,
Our love, a garden to behold,
In every bloom, our lives unfold.

The Dance of Hearts

Beneath the moon's enchanting light,
Two hearts embark on love's soft flight,
In rhythm, steps both bold and bright,
A dance that swirls through day and night.

With every touch, a spark ignites,
As laughter fills the starry nights,
In this embrace, the world's delights,
Are captured in our soaring kites.

In the ballroom's grace or forest's shade,
In meadows where the sunlight played,
Our hearts winded in steps portrayed,
A dance where memories are made.

Through waltz's sweep and tango's fire,
In every sway, a deep desire,
To feel the music's gentle lyre,
On every note, our hearts aspire.

In slow dances beneath the trees,
In quick steps with the ocean breeze,
Our love's a dance that brings such ease,
In every twirl, we find the keys.

When night descends with quiet grace,
In silent halls, we find our place,
In whispered tunes, in close embrace,
Our hearts still dance, in time and space.

Through every rhythm, soft or wild,
In tempos fast, in measures mild,
Our souls unite, no longer tiled,
A dance that renders us beguiled.

With every dawn, we find the beat,
In every dusk, the rhythm sweet,
Our love's a dance, complete, replete,
In every step, our hearts repeat.

In moments when the music slows,
In crescendos where passion grows,
Our love's a dance that always knows,
In harmony, through highs and lows.

With feet in sync and hands entwined,
In love's great dance, our hearts combined,
In every waltz, in every find,
A rhythm true, by fate design

A Whisper's Kiss

In shadows where secrets hide,
Our love, a whisper, side by side,
With every kiss, the fears subside,
In each other, we confide.

Through silent nights and echoed morn,
Our spirits intertwine, reborn,
A gentle touch, a promise sworn,
Together, facing every storm.

In quiet rooms where shadows fall,
Our whispered love surpasses all,
Through every echo, every call,
Our hearts unite, both large and small.

With silent glances, eyes that gleam,
In murmured words, a shared dream,
Our love, a steady, flowing stream,
In whispers, we become a team.

In the hush of night, where shadows creep,
In dreams that linger, thoughts run deep,
Our love, a bond, a vow to keep,
In whispers, where our hearts can leap.

Through every sigh, through every breeze,
In moments still, where time can freeze,
Our love persists in tender pleas,
In whispers, we find lasting ease.

In rooms of quiet, peace and calm,
In silences that hold a balm,
Our hearts find solace, sweet and warm,
In whispers, we find our arm.

With every glance, a secret shared,
In every look, a soul laid bare,
Our whispered love, beyond compare,
In silence, showing how we care.

Through echoes of a love so true,
In whispered tones, our hearts renew,
A bond that grows in shadows' view,
In whispers, where our spirits flew.

In quiet moments, hearts confess,
In every whispered soft caress,
Our Love's a song of pure finesse,
In silence, we embrace the rest.

Echoes of Our Song

On rivers where echoes play,
Our Love's a song that finds its way,
Through notes that drift at break of the day,
In melodies that softly sway.

With every chord, a memory,
Of laughter shared beneath the tree,
In harmony, just you and me,
Our hearts compose love's symphony.

In gentle streams where currents flow,
Our Love's a song that softly grows,
In rhythms where the breezes blow,
In echoes where our hearts bestow.

Through melodies of joy and pain,
In notes that fall like summer rain,
Our love's a song that does not wane,
In every chorus, a pure refrain.

With every verse, a story told,
Of moments cherished, ages old,
In harmonies both soft and bold,
Our hearts echo bright and gold.

In symphonies of night and day,
In crescendos that find their way,
Our love's a tune that will not sway,
In every note, we find our stay.

Through whispers of a gentle song,
In echoes where our hearts belong,
Our love endures, so pure and strong,
In melodies that can't go wrong.

In every lyric, pure and sweet,
In every rhythm, our hearts meet,
A song where souls and spirits greet,
In echoes where love is complete.

With every chord that strings align,
In harmonies where hearts combine,
Our love's a song, both yours and mine,
In echoes where our souls entwine.

In rivers where echoes play,
Our Love's a song that lights the way,
In every note and every lay,
In echoes where our hearts display.

The Bridge We Build

Between the stars and endless sea,
We build a bridge from you to me,
With trust and hope, our destiny,
A path where only love can be.

With every step, the future gleams,
In golden hues of whispered dreams,
Our lives are entwined in flowing streams,
Connected by the light that throws the beams.

In every arch, a promise made,
In every span, hope displayed,
Our love's a bridge that will not fade,
In strength and faith, we are arrayed.

Through storms that shake and winds that bend,
In every test, we depend,
Our bond's a bridge that does not end,
In every trial, we transcend.

With every stone, a story laid,
Of journeys shared, of fears allayed,
Our love, a bridge that does not trade,
In every challenge, unafraid.

Between the night and dawning day,
Our bridge of love finds its way,
In shadows cast and light's array,
A path that leads where hearts can stay

In every span, our hearts embrace,
In every step, we find our place,
A bridge that time will not erase,
In love's pure light, in endless grace.

Through valleys deep and mountains high,
In every tear and every sigh,
Our bridge of love reaches the sky,
In every moment, we comply.

Between the stars and endless sea,
Our bridge of love sets spirits free,
A path where only we can see,
In every step, our hearts agree.

In Silence We Speak

In quiet rooms where shadows fall,
Our love persists beyond the wall,
In silence, we can hear the call,
A bond that rises above all.

With tender glances, words unseen,
In simple gestures, love is gleaned,
Through every whisper in between,
Our hearts convey what words can't mean.

In moments where the world is still,
In silence, our spirits thrill,
A bond that grows, both firm and real,
In every look, our hearts reveal.

In echoes soft where shadows blend,
In silence, our souls ascend,
A love that silence cannot amend,
At every glance, we comprehend.

Through every hush, our hearts unite,
In silences where stars ignite,
Our love endures beyond the night,
In whispered dreams,

Nostalgia

The Echoes of Yesteryear

In corners where the shadows blend,
The echoes of our past ascend,
A song of days that never end,
In memories where hearts still tend.

Through alleys where our laughter played,
In sunlight where our secrets stayed,
In whispers soft, in voices laid,
The echoes of our youth are portrayed.

We danced in fields where daisies grew,
In summer's warmth, in skies so blue,
With every breeze, our spirits flew,
In memories, our dreams renew.

In winter when the snow falls,
By cosy hearths and childhood halls,
In echoes of a distant call,
Our past returns, both large and small.

In every scent of autumn's grace,
In every leaf that finds its place,
The echoes of our past embrace,
Moments that time cannot erase.

Through photo albums, pages turned,
In faded ink where stories burned,
The echoes of our youth returned,
In memories, where love is learned.

In whispers of the dawn's first light,
In twilight where the stars ignite,
The echoes of our past take flight,
In gentle hues of day and night.

In every song that brings a smile,
In every path, we walked a mile,
The echoes of our past compile,
In tender thoughts that reconcile.

In dreams that linger, soft and true,
In memories where we renew,
The echoes of our past ensue,
In quiet moments, just we two.

Through every sigh, through every tear,
In laughter's light and shadow's fear,
The echoes of our yesteryear,
Remain within, forever near

The Roads Once Wandered

In corners where the shadows blend,
The echoes of our past ascend,
A song of days that never end,
In memories where hearts still tend.

Through alleys where our laughter played,
In sunlight where our secrets stayed,
In whispers soft, in voices laid,
The echoes of our youth are portrayed.

We danced in fields where daisies grew,
In summer's warmth, in skies so blue,
With every breeze, our spirits flew,
In memories, our dreams renew.

In winter when the snow falls,
By cosy hearths and childhood halls,
In echoes of a distant call,
Our past returns, both large and small.

In every scent of autumn's grace,
In every leaf that finds its place,
The echoes of our past embrace,
Moments that time cannot erase.

Through photo albums, pages turned,
In faded ink where stories burned,
The echoes of our youth returned,
In memories, where love is learned.

In whispers of the dawn's first light,
In twilight where the stars ignite,
The echoes of our past take flight,
In gentle hues of day and night.

In every song that brings a smile,
In every path, we walked a mile,
The echoes of our past compile,
In tender thoughts that reconcile.

In dreams that linger, soft and true,
In memories where we renew,
The echoes of our past ensue,
In quiet moments, just we two.

Through every sigh, through every tear,
In laughter's light and shadow's fear,
The echoes of our yesteryear,
Remain within, forever near

Childhood's Embrace

In fields where childhood dreams did play,
In sunlight where we lost the day,
In laughter where the shadows lay,
Our memories, in a bright array.

Through gardens where the flowers grew,
In whispers where the breezes blew,
In moments that our hearts renew,
Our childhood dreams return to view.

In swings where once we touched the sky,
In kites that flew so high,
In every laugh, in every sigh,
Our childhood spirit passes by.

In winter when the snow would fall,
In summer when the birds would call,
In autumn's gold, in springtime's thrall,
Our childhood's grace, we still recall.

Through days when sunshine warmed our face,
On nights where stars found their place,
In memories, we find the trace,
Of childhood's soft, enduring grace.

In games where once we ran so free,
In hide and seek beneath the tree,
In every glance, in every spree,
Our childhood's joys are a guarantee.

In whispered tales of knights and queens,
In stories told in twilight scenes,
In every shadow, every beam,
Our childhood's dreams forever gleam.

Through every dawn and every dusk,
In every laugh, in every trust,
Our childhood memories adjust,
To moments where our hearts combust.

In echoes of a distant call,
In dreams where we were once so small,
Our childhood's grace, we still recall,
In every step, in every fall.

In fields where childhood dreams did play,
In laughter where the shadows lay,
our memories in bright arrays
Return to light in the present day.

The Lanterns of Time

In lanterns where the light would glow,
In evenings when the past would show,
In memories that softly flow,
Our hearts return to long ago.

Through corridors where shadows blend,
In whispers where the echoes bend,
In lanterns lit, where dreams ascend,
Our memories, like lights, extend.

In alleys where the twilight falls,
In whispers where the night recalls,
In lanterns bright, within the halls,
Our memories, the past enthralls.

In every flicker, every gleam,
In moments when our spirits dream,
In lanterns where the memories stream,
Our hearts find solace in the beam.

Through days when sunlight kissed the land,
On nights when stars would understand,
In lanterns lit by gentle hands,
Our memories, a sacred band.

In shadows where the past resides,
In corners where our love abides,
In lanterns where the light provides,
A bridge where time and space collides.

In every glow, in every ray,
In moments where our hearts would stay,
In lanterns where the night finds day,
Our memories, a warm display.

Through every year, through every age,
In moments where the memories wage,
In lanterns lit, where hearts engage,
Our past returns, a sacred page.

In lanterns where the light would glow,
In evenings when the past would show,
In memories that softly flow,
Our hearts return to long ago.

The Scent of Yesterday

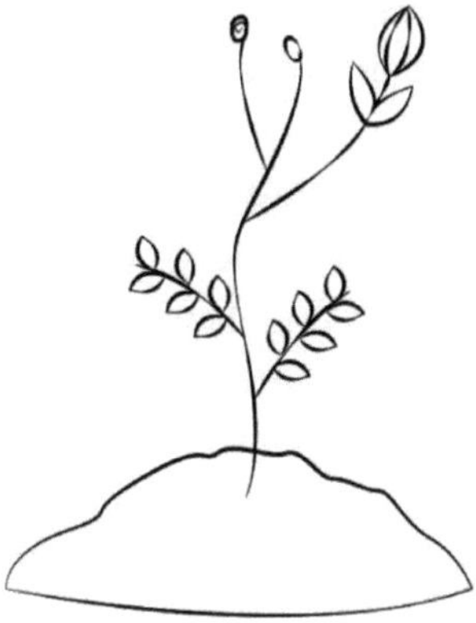

In gardens where the lilies bloom,
In twilight where the shadows loom,
In scents that linger in the room,
Our memories return to bloom.

Through fields where lavender would grow,
In breezes where the flowers show,
In scents that carry whispers low,
Our past returns, a gentle flow.

In kitchens where the spices blend,
In fragrances where moments bend,
In scents that carry, dreams extend,
Our hearts return, the past to mend.

Through days when jasmine filled the air,
On nights when roses bloomed so fair,
In scents that linger everywhere,
Our memories, beyond compare.

In whispers of a springtime's grace,
In echoes where the summers chase,
In scents that find their own embrace,
Our hearts return, the past retrace.

Through autumn's leaves, in winters cold,
In scents of cedar, ages old,
In every scent, our hearts behold,
The memories where love is told.

In perfumes where the roses blend,
In lilacs where the dreams ascend,
In scents that carry, hearts amend,
Our past returns, as time extends.

Through every scent that lingers still,
In fragrances where hearts fulfill,
In scents that carry, soft and shrill,
Our memories return, at will.

In gardens where the lilies bloom,
In twilight where the shadows loom,
In scents that linger in the room,
Our memories return to bloom.

The Touch of Bygone Days

In touches where the past resides,
In moments where the heart abides,
In memories where love confides,
Our hearts return to bygone tides.

Through hands that once did hold so tight,
In whispers of a love's delight,
In touches where the past ignites,
Our memories, in soft invite.

In hugs where warmth would never fade,
In hands that held in times displayed,
In touches where the past is laid,
Our hearts return, the present swayed.

Through gestures where the love was shown,
In moments where the seeds were sown,
In touches where the past is known,
Our memories, a gentle loan.

In every glance, in every hold,
In touches where the past unfolds,
Our hearts return to tales retold,
In memories, where love is bold.

Through hands that worked and hands that played,
In touches where the heart conveyed,
In memories where love displayed,
Our hearts return, the past portrayed.

In every clasp, in every squeeze,
In touches where the past would please,
Our hearts return to times of ease,
In memories, like gentle seas.

Through touches where the love remains,
In gestures where the heart sustains,
In memories where love refrains,
Our hearts return to soft campaigns.

In touches where the past resides,
In moments where the heart abides,
In memories where love confides,
Our hearts return to bygone tides.

Technology's Impact

The Digital Tide

In seas where signals ebb and flow,
And currents of data brightly glow,
Our lives, transformed, in future shows,
By waves of change, we come to know.

In pixels where our visions gleam,
In screens that light the darkest dream,
The digital tide, a living stream,
Where bytes and bits fulfill a scheme.

Through wires where our voices blend,
And whispers of messages send,
The digital tide, without an end,
In every link, our lives extend.

In clouds where memories abide,
In networks where our worlds collide,
The digital tide, our modern guide,
Through waves, our hearts find places to hide.

Algorithms weave and decide,
In cryptic codes where secrets bide,
The digital tide, deep inside,
In every beat, our lives reside.

Each tap and click, in rapid ticks,
In every scroll, where rhythm flicks,
The digital tide, a magic mix,
In every pulse, our hearts do fix.

Where data flows and knowledge grows,
In realms where only numbers know,
The digital tide, in highs and lows,
Shows the path where futures go.

Where voices merge and worlds converge,
In endless data streams that surge,
The digital tide, in its great urge,
In every wave, our hearts emerge.

Through optic threads and satellite lights,
In glowing screens of endless nights,
The digital tide, both days and nights,
With every spark, our future writes.

In oceans where the signals flow,
Through currents where the data glow,
Our lives, transformed, the future's show,
By waves of change, we come to know

The Clockwork Rhythm

In gears where time and circuits blend,
Where future shines and pathways wend,
Our lives entwine in digital trends,
With clockwork rhythm, hearts ascend.

In silent gears that turn with grace,
In microchips where pulses trace,
The clockwork rhythm sets the pace,
In every beat, our hearts embrace.

In silicon where thoughts reside,
Where pulses spark and worlds collide,
The clockwork rhythm, deep inside,
In every tick, our lives abide.

With binary codes and numbers flow,
In algorithms where pathways show,
The clockwork rhythm, futures stow,
In every line, our hearts bestow.

In screens where visions come to play,
In data streams of night and day,
The clockwork rhythm finds its way,
In every byte, our dreams convey.

Through circuits where the signals race,
In networks where our thoughts embrace,
The clockwork rhythm, endless chase,
In every pulse, our hearts retrace.

In chips where knowledge does reside,
In memories where data hides,
The clockwork rhythm, our guide,
In every beat, our lives reside.

In wires where voices hum a tune,
In echoes where futures loom,
The clockwork rhythm, steady boom,
In every note, our hearts attune

In systems where the codes align,
Where frameworks and the futures shine,
The clockwork rhythm, hearts combine,
In every pulse, a grand design.

In gears where time and circuits blend,
Where future shines and pathways wend,
Our lives entwine in digital trends,
With clockwork rhythm, hearts ascend

The Virtual Embrace

In worlds where pixels shape the scene,
Where shadows lean and light is keen,
Our lives embrace the virtual sheen,
With screens and codes, our hearts convene.

Through lenses where our visions play,
In virtual realms where dreams convey,
Our hearts connect in digital sway,
In every frame, a bright array.

In spaces where codes intertwine,
In realms where only data shines,
The virtual embrace defines,
In every touch, our hearts combine.

Through avatars where voices speak,
In pixels where our spirits seek,
The virtual embrace, unique,
In every byte, our hearts bespeak.

In networks where signals blend,
In virtual worlds where messages send,
Our hearts in virtual embrace extend,
In every line, our lives ascend.

Through screens where laughter, tears, and glee,
In pixels where our spirits free,
The virtual embrace, a key,
In every wave, our hearts agree.

In realms where dreams become the light,
In pixels where the days unite,
Our hearts in virtual embrace alight,
In every click, our futures write.

Through codes where information flows,
In virtual worlds where data grows,
The virtual embrace shows,
In every pulse, our hearts disclose.

In networks where the distances close,
In virtual realms where only light shows,
Our hearts in virtual embrace pose,
In every byte, our dreams compose.

In worlds where pixels shape the scene,
Where shadows lean and light is keen,
Our lives embrace the virtual sheen,
With screens and codes, our hearts convene.

Simplicity and complexities

The Essence of Simplicity

In a world of tangles, intricate weave,
Lies a truth we often leave:
A simple breath, a gentle breeze,
The essence of life's simple ease.

Amid chaos, where the mind does strain,
In webs of thought where complexities reign,
In calm and silence, where peace maintains,
The heart finds joy in simple gains.

The sun rises with golden light,
The moon glows in the quiet night.
These simple things, devoid of fight,
Bring warmth and joy, pure delight.

A single flower in a field of green,
A child's laughter, fresh and keen,
In these moments, we clearly glean,
The simple joys, forever seen.

In simple words, the heart can share,
In gentle smiles beyond compare,
Complexities fade when love lays bare,
In simple acts, we show we care.

The taste of bread, the sip of tea,
In these, we find simplicity.
A life lived with humility
Brings contentment, truly free.

For in the simple lies the key
To live life with clarity.
In every breath, each decree,
Simplicity brings serenity.

So let's pause in life's busy swirl,
And find joy in the simple twirl.
For in simplicity, the truth unfurls:
A peaceful heart in a complex world

The Dance of Complexity

In tangled webs where thoughts reside,
In labyrinths where secrets hide,
Complexities in life abide—
A dance of chaos deep inside.

Through twists and turns, the pathways lead,
In shadows where the heart may bleed,
Complexities plant their seed
In every thought, in every deed.

In systems vast, in networks spread,
In tangled codes that fill our heads,
Complexities where dreams are fed
In every choice, in every thread.

The dance of thoughts, a frantic pace,
In every problem, every case,
Complexities show a daunting face
In every heart, in every space.

Yet in tangled minds' intricate weave,
Where chaos reigns and order grieves,
A deeper truth and rhythm leave
A path where complexities ease.

For every twist, there's strength to gain;
In every knot, a lesson plain.
Complexities, though they strain,
Reveal the beauty in the pain.

Through patterns rich and textures deep,
In complexities where secrets keep,
The dance unfolds, a mind's leap
In every beat where hearts do steep.

In chaos where shadows blend,
In complexities that never end,
A harmony does transcend—
In every twist, the truths ascend.

So let's dance in tangled lines,
In complexities where light combines.
For in chaos, beauty shines:
A deeper truth the heart defines.

The Harmony

In a world of paradox, wide and vast,
Where simple joys and complex cast,
There lies a harmony unsurpassed—
In simplicity and complexity, a dance amassed.

A leaf that falls in autumn air,
In simple grace, without a care,
Yet in its veins, complexities share
A story of life beyond compare.

A child's gaze in wonder bright,
In simple awe of nature's sight,
Yet behind those eyes, complexities fight
To understand the world's might.

The rhythm of waves on a quiet shore,
A simple pulse in nature's core,
Yet in the deep, complexities roar
In currents where the unknown explores.

The song of a bird in morning light,
In simple notes that take their flight,
Yet in each call, complexities write
A melody of life's delight.

In every heart, a simple beat,
A rhythm where the pulses meet,
Yet in each throb, complexities fleet—
A dance where life and love compete.

The turning of the seasons' wheel,
In simple cycles, clear and real,
Yet in each change, complexities reveal
A tapestry of life's appeal.

So in the blend of simple and deep,
Where complexities and calm do seep,
There lies a harmony we keep
In every thought, in every leap.

For in the simple and the grand,
In complexities we understand
The beauty of life's woven strand—
A harmony that does expand.

So let's embrace both near and far,
In simplicity and complex spar,
For in this dance, we truly are
A harmony beneath the stars.

Tradition and Change

The Echo of Tradition

In the hearth where embers glow,
Where ancient fires gently flow,
Tradition's voice, both soft and low,
Whispers tales from long ago.

In every grain, the hands that knead,
In rituals where hearts do feed,
Tradition, like an ancient creed,
Guides us in our every need.

In dances where the rhythms beat,
In songs where voices, old and sweet,
Tradition's echoes softly meet
In melodies both calm and fleet.

Yet in the winds, a change does stir,
A whisper in the distant blur.
Tradition bends and starts to purr
In breaths where future dreams occur.

In looms where patterns blend,
In threads where past and present mend,
Tradition yields but does defends
Its essence in each woven end.

In every toast, in every cheer,
In rituals that hold us near,
Tradition's presence remains clear,
Even as the new appears.

Through corridors of time we walk,
In shadows where the past does talk,
Tradition blends in every clock,
With changes that the new unlocks.

In fields where new seeds take root,
In songs where modern voices hoot,
Tradition and change, in pursuit,
Of harmony where hearts salute.

For in each tale, in every hand,
Tradition guides where we do stand.
Yet change reshapes as hearts expand,
Together in a woven strand.

So let us honor what is old,
In traditions that our hearts hold,
Yet welcome change in gentle fold,
For both in unity are bold.

The Winds of Change

On hills where ancient trees have grown,
In fields where only time has sown,
Tradition stands, a presence known
In every root, in every stone.

Through pathways where our fathers walked,
In shadows where old voices talked,
Tradition's echo softly stalked
In every tale, in every thought.

Yet in the breeze, a wind does rise,
In whispers where the future flies.
Tradition bends as change applies
Its breath beneath the open skies.

In cities where the new lights shine,
In streets where modern voices chime,
Tradition sways, begins to climb,
With change's rhythm, new in time.

For every leaf that falls away,
In seasons where the old does sway,
Tradition yields, begins to play
With change's dawn, a new array.

In temples where the old prayers sing,
In marketplaces where new ideas spring,
Tradition and change, their voices ring,
In harmony, a shared offering.

In every art, in every craft,
In bridges where the past does raft,
Tradition weaves, with change's shaft,
A tapestry both old and daft.

So let the winds of change blow clear,
In breaths where futures do appear,
For in their dance, both far and near,
Tradition blends without a fear.

In every heart, in every tale,
Tradition and change both set sail,
Together in the winds prevail,
In life's grand journey, without fail

The Embrace of New and Old

In courtyards where the stories start,
In rituals where the old impart,
Tradition holds a sacred part
In every hand, in every heart.

Through songs where ancient voices blend,
In dances where the old extend,
Tradition's line does gently bend
In steps that never truly end.

In kitchens where old spices lay,
In festivals that light the way,
Tradition guides, both night and day,
In every feast, in every play.

Yet on the horizon, a dawn unfolds,
In whispers where the future molds.
Tradition meets the new that holds,
In hands where modern warmth enfolds.

In classrooms where young minds explore,
In workshops where new ideas soar,
Tradition and change, in thoughts galore,
Combine to open every door.

For in the old, the new does spring,
In echoes where the future sings.
Tradition bends, begins to bring
A blend where change and past do cling.

In every bridge that spans the way,
In paths where new meets old halfway,
Tradition and change, in bright array,
Embrace each step in soft ballet.

Through every thread in life's great loom,
In gardens where both old and new bloom,
Tradition weaves with change's plume
A story where both light and room.

So let us honor what has been
In traditions where our hearts have seen,
Yet welcome change, where futures lean,
Together in life's woven sheen.

For in the blend of new and old,
A tale of harmony is told.
Tradition and change, together bold,
In hearts where life's true lights unfold

MOTHER

The Eternal Embrace

In the early dawn, where morning's new,
And dew still clings to fields and leaves,
A mother's love shines pure and true,
A melody the heart believes.

With hands that cradle tender dreams,
And words that soothe the silent night,
A mother's touch, like moonlit beams,
Guides us gently into light.

Her eyes reflect the endless skies,
A mirror of the love she gives,
In every hug and every sigh,
Her spirit in each heartbeat lives.

Through years of joy and heartfelt tears,
In moments bright and quiet still,
A mother's love, beyond all fears,
A steady warmth time cannot kill.

She lifts the weight from heavy days,
Her strength in every step we find,
A beacon through the darkest maze,
Her courage in our hearts enshrined.

In her embrace, the world feels right,
Her whispers where solace grows,
A mother's love, a constant light,
In her presence, true peace flows.

Her smile brings hope’s return each day,
In every word, a lesson’s told,
A mother’s love, a fire that stays,
Through winter’s cold, through autumn’s gold.

As years turn gold, in lines and care,
Her love, forever bold and fine,
A timeless truth beyond compare,
A mother's love, a love divine.

So hold her close, both far and near,
In every breath, in every tear,
A mother’s love, forever dear,
An eternal embrace, always here

The Heart's Anchor

In seas where tempests rage and roar,
In waves where darkness hides the shore,
A mother stands, a steadfast core,
An anchor where our hearts restore.

Her arms, a haven warm and safe,
In storms where fears and doubts perform,
A mother's love, a gentle wave,
Where every heart finds calm reborn.

Through every trial, every plight,
In battles where we lose our sight,
A mother's love, a guiding light,
Through shadows deep, through darkest nights.

In lullabies that soothe the soul,
In stories where our dreams unfold,
A mother's words, so sweet and bold,
Shape our hearts in gentle mold.

Her laughter, like a summer breeze,
Brings moments where the heart finds ease,
A mother's joy in times of peace,
In every smile, in every tease.

Through seasons where the leaves do fall,
In winters when the cold does call,
A mother's love, above it all,
A warmth that never does forestall.

In every tear and every laugh,
In every wound where love does graft,
A mother's love, a healing craft,
A soothing balm, a gentle draft.

As days blend into years we send,
In memories where love extends,
A mother's heart, a faithful friend,
A constant love that has no end.

In every night, in every day,
Her love, a light to guide our way,
A mother's love, in bright array,
An anchor where our souls will stay.

The Symphony of Love

In the gentle notes of morning's rise,
Where the day begins with soft sighs,
A mother's voice, like a lullaby,
Whispers where love's roots lie.

Her touch, a symphony so tender,
In every chord where joys wander,
A mother's love, a warm surrender,
In each note, a lasting splendour.

Through melodies where dreams take flight,
In harmonies that guide through night,
A mother's song, a gentle light,
In every heart, a beacon bright.

Her laughter, like the sun's warm gleam,
In whispered hopes where futures dream,
A mother's love, a steady theme,
In every wish, a guiding beam.

Her smile, a dawn amidst a storm,
Her hug, a place that's always warm,
A mother's heart, a nurturing norm,
In every gesture, love takes form.

Through symphonies of life's grand song,
In rhythms where we all belong,
A mother's love, enduring, strong,
In every heart, it sings along.

In times when joy and sorrow blend,
When life's paths twist and wend,
A mother's love, a constant friend,
In every note, a strength to mend.

Let the music of her heart,
In every life, in every part,
A mother's love, a work of art,
In each beat, a loving start.

For in her song, we find our way,
Through night and day, come what may,
A mother's love, in bright array,
A symphony that forever stays.

DIVERSE FACET OF LIFE

Journey to Kaziranga

In Assam's heart, where rivers wind,
And emerald fields with beauty bind,
Lies Kaziranga, wild and grand,
A treasure in this timeless land.

We ventured forth at the break of dawn,
Where misty light on grass was drawn,
Through morning's hush and fragrant air,
The promise of adventure there.

The jungle's song in whispers rose,
Through ancient trees where nature knows,
With rustling leaves and rivers' call,
A symphony where wild dreams sprawl.

The one-horned rhino, regal, proud,
In grassy fields, alone, unbowed,
A creature of majestic might,
In shadowed woods and morning light.

Through bamboo groves and silver streams,
In Kaziranga's vibrant dreams,
We caught a glimpse of tigers rare,
Their amber eyes and golden glare.

In Orchid Park, a bloom of hues,
Where nature's palette brightly strews,
A garden of the rarest kind,
In petals where the spirits find.

The orchids danced in colors wild,
In every blossom, nature smiled,
A tapestry of life's own grace,
In Kaziranga's tranquil space.

We journeyed on through forests deep,
Where hidden wonders softly sleep,
The river Brahmaputra's flow,
In sunlight's tender, golden glow.

Elephants in gentle stride,
Through marshes green where secrets hide,
And deer that leapt in graceful bounds,
Through silent woods and open grounds.

The sunset bathed the land in gold,
Where every heart a story told,
In Kaziranga's warm embrace,
We found a world of endless grace.

As nightfall drew its velvet veil,
And stars began their timeless tale,
We left with hearts forever changed,
By nature's beauty, unrestrained.

In Kaziranga, wild and free,
A world of life's own poetry,
Where rhinos roam and tigers prowl,
In forests where the spirits howl.

So let us cherish every scene,
In Kaziranga's realms serene,
A testament to nature's care,
A paradise beyond compare.

The Enchantment of Her Presence

In the garden where twilight sings,
Where shadows dance and night brings,
She stands, a queen, where beauty springs,
In echoes where the evening clings.

Her hair, a river dark and deep,
Flows like silk where shadows sleep,
Below her shoulders, soft and steep,
A whisper where the night winds sweep.

Her eyes, two lotus blossoms bright,
Shine like stars in velvet night,
A radiant glow, a beacon light,
Where dreams are born in endless flight.

Her skin, a satin canvas fair,
Smooth as whispers in the air,
A touch of silk beyond compare,
In twilight's glow, beyond all care.

She moves as if the world's her own,
In every step, a regal tone,
Her walk, a queen upon her throne,
In grace where beauty's essence's shown.

Her laughter, like a brook's sweet song,
A melody that carries strong,
In every note, where hearts belong,
A rhythm where all joys prolong.

With every step on the ground,
In every glance where lights abound,
Her beauty's where true grace is found,
In every echo, sweet and round.

Her smile, a sunrise softly traced,
A warmth within twilight's taste,
In every curve, where hearts embraced,
A light that no time can erase.

Her presence, like a dream's sweet thread,
In every word, in things unsaid,
A vision where the heart is led,
In paths where purest dreams are bred.

In twilight's dance, in moonlit air,
Where shadows play and stars do stare,
Her beauty shines beyond compare,
A vision where the heart lays bare

A Vision of Radiance

In the soft light of morning's grace, she stands,
A vision of beauty that quietly commands,
Her black hair flows in silky strands,
Like the night's own velvet through her hands.

Her eyes, dark and luminous like lotus blooms,
Hold secrets where the stars find room,
A playful glimmer, dispelling gloom,
Where dreams and laughter leave their mark.

Her skin, smooth as moonlight's glow,
Where shadows dance and whispers flow,
A canvas where the roses grow,
In hues that only angels know.

She walks as if the world's her stage,
Each step a turn of a poetic page,
With every glance, a heart's new rage,
In a dance where beauty does engage.

Her laughter, a bell so sweet and clear,
A melody where joy draws near,
Each note a rhythmic beat we hear,
A song that makes the heart repeat.

With grace that lights the twilight's seam,
Each movement like a dancer's dream,
She walks where beauty's rivers gleam,
In ripples of pure elegance.

Her smile, a dawn in twilight's hush,
A bloom within the evening's blush,
In every curve, a tender rush,
Where hearts and souls begin to flush.

Her presence, like a gentle breeze,
In whispers where the lilies tease,
A symphony where spirits ease,
A moment where all sorrows cease.

In the dance of stars and moonlit skies,
In the echoes where the night wind flies,
Her beauty shines where truth lies,
A vision where the heart complies.

So in her gaze, the world does find,
A beauty that transcends the mind,
In every breath, a love refined,
A treasure where our dreams unwind.

The Symphony of Her Beauty

In the dawn where sunlight beams,
Where morning wakes from silken dreams,
She stands, a vision where beauty streams,
In whispers where elegance teems.

Her hair, a cascade soft and dark,
Falls like shadows in a park,
Below her shoulders, leaving a mark,
A touch of night in morning's spark.

Her eyes, like lotuses in bloom,
In twilight's hush and evening's gloom,
Shine with a light that brightens the room,
A radiance that dispels all the doom.

Her skin, a canvas smooth and bright,
As soft as whispers in the night,
A glow within the softest light,
A touch of union of day and night.

She moves with grace, a dancer's flair,
Each step a breath of tender air,
Her walk, a song beyond compare,
A dance where beauty's threads are fair.

Her laughter, like a songbird's call,
A melody that graces all,
In every note, a rise, a fall,
A rhythm where true joys enthrall.

With every glance, a tale unfolds,
In every smile, a warmth that holds,
Her beauty in the morning molds,
A vision where true grace extols.

Her smile, a dawn where love does wake,
A sunrise on a morning lake,
In every curve, where hearts partake,
A joy that no sorrow can shake.

Her presence, like a gentle breeze,
In whispers where the night agrees,
A symphony where hearts find ease,
A melody that never flees.

In every step, in every sight,
In mornings where the world's alight,
Her beauty shines with pure delight,
A vision where the heart takes flight.

So let her grace and beauty flow,
In dawn's embrace, where day does grow,
Her essence in the morning glow,
A symphony where hearts bestow.

A Dainty Dance of Blossoms

In gardens where the morning dew
Bathes dainty blossoms, freshly new,
Their petals touched by gentle light,
A symphony of colors bright.

A butterfly with wings so fine
Dances around the twisting vine,
Its movements, delicate and pure,
In this enchanted world, demure.

Amid the whispers of the breeze,
The dainty flowers sway with ease,
Their fragrance floats on gentle air,
A scent so sweet, beyond compare.

So let us pause and deeply savor
The beauty of each subtle flavor,
For in life's tapestry, they blend,
With elegance, their grace extends.

Whispering Rainfall

In the hush of night when stars softly gleam,
The world finds peace in a tranquil dream.
A gentle patter, rhythmic and calm,
Rain whispers a lullaby, a soothing balm.

Through windowpanes, it tells a tale,
Of nature's dance, a waltz without fail.
Each drop, a story, each rhythm, a song,
In the symphony of rain, we all belong.

It cleanses the earth with a tender touch,
Reviving the soul, healing so much.
In every droplet, a promise of grace,
Painting the world in silver lace.

Amidst the misty veil of midnight rain,
Two hearts entwined in love's sweet refrain.
Whispering beneath the moon's soft glow,
They find a love only raindrops know.

Hand in hand, beneath the silver sky,
They walk, lost in each other, as the world
passes by.
Their love, like rain, falls in gentle streams,
A symphony of passion within their dreams.

So let it fall and wash away
The worries and woes of every day.
For in the gentle rain's embrace,
We find peace amidst life's constant race.

Innocence Remembered

In the gentle embrace of memory's glow,
Where time's gentle whispers softly flow,
There lies a canvas woven in youth,
Of fleeting romances and love's sweet truth.

In the golden hues of dawn's first light,
We danced in the shadows, hearts taking flight.
Infatuation's spell, a tender embrace,
Painted our world with passion and grace.

Oh, to wander once more in that dream,
Where love's tender whispers gleam.
In the garden of youth, where innocence blooms,
We found solace in love's sweet perfumes.

But time, like a river, flows ever on,
And the echoes of youth become distant and
gone.
Yet in the depths of our hearts, they remain,
A cherished memory, a lingering refrain.

So let us raise a toast to the days of yore,
To the love we knew and the dreams we bore.
For though the years may pass and fade away,
The echoes of youth forever shall stay.

In the quiet moments, in the still of the night,
We'll remember the laughter, the love, and the light.
For in the grand carpet of life's grand design,
Youthful romances forever intertwine.

Welcoming Spring

In Spring's embrace, love blooms anew,
As nature's canvas paints the view.
A symphony of colours bright,
In petals soft, love takes its flight.

In fields of green, where flowers sway,
Two hearts entwine in gentle play.
Beneath the azure, endless sky,
Their love unfolds, no need to pry.

With whispers carried on the breeze,
They find solace beneath the trees.
Hand in hand, they roam the glade,
In Spring's embrace, their fears evade.

Each dawn reveals a world reborn,
Where love's sweet song is softly sworn.
In fragrant meadows, they explore,
Their passion kindled evermore.

As sunbeams dance upon their skin,
Their souls entwine, no need to win.
For in this season, love is free,
Bound by nature's sweet decree.

So let us cherish Spring's embrace,
And bask in love's enchanting grace.
For in its bloom, we find our truth,
In Spring's embrace, eternal youth.

Holi Festivity

In Barpeta's heart, where greenery thrives,
Doul Utsav blooms, and joy arrives.
Riya dances, her laughter so bright,
In the festival's glow, all burdens take flight.

With dawn's gentle kiss, the town awakes,
Adorning courtyards with flowers and flakes.
Intricate rangolis, colors ablaze,
Whisper tales of joy in vibrant displays.

As drums beat and melodies soar,
Through the streets, traditions adore.
In Assamese attire, with hearts light as air,
They sing and dance, making a jubilant affair.

Young and old, all souls unite,
In the kaleidoscope of colors, no divide in sight.
Faces painted with hues, a rainbow's embrace,
Symbolizing togetherness, love's warm grace.

Underneath the sky as colors fly,
Vaishnavite hymns blend, reaching high.
In Barpeta's heart, Vaishnavite culture thrives,
Amidst the joyous revelry, its essence arrives.

Holi songs echo, their tunes so sweet,
Adding rhythm to the festivities' beat.
Voices rise in unison, hearts overflow,
With love and joy, their spirits aglow.

As the sun bows down and bonfires light,
Holika's demise, virtue's flight.
Prayers rise, a chorus of hope and cheer,
Echoing in the tranquil atmosphere.

In Barpeta's embrace, Riya sees,
A tapestry of culture where love's breeze.
Doul Utsav's hues, a symphony of glee,
A celebration of unity, for all to see.

As night descends and laughter fades,
Riya knows, in her heart, what Doul Utsav makes.
A legacy of joy, unity's song,
In Barpeta's embrace, where all belong.

Note:
Barpeta is a township in Assam, India, with a rich heritage of Vaishnavite culture. Holi is celebrated each year with all rituals and fanfare.

Butterfly

In gardens kissed by morning light,
A butterfly takes graceful flight.
Its wings adorned with colors bold,
A story of connection told.

Like fragile wings that flutter by,
Our lives are but a fleeting sigh.
Yet in the dance of time's ballet,
whisper in the morning sky.

The butterfly, a symbol of bright,
Of transformation, taking a flight.
Its journey mirrors our quest,
To find ourselves, to be our best.

In every flutter, every glide,
A tale of beauty cannot hide.
For in its delicate embrace,
We see reflections of our grace.

So let us cherish, hand in hand,
The bond between this wondrous land.
For in the butterfly's fleeting span,
We find a connection between women and men.

In nature's dance, we find our part,
A beating of the human heart.
United in this cosmic flow,
Like butterflies, we come and go.

The Natures Music

In fields adorned with hues anew,
Spring whispers secrets, old yet true.
Where trees unfurl their emerald sheen,
And morning's symphony, the koel's unseen.

Let us welcome, with hearts aglow,
As springtime's magic begins to sow.
In this season of hope and cheer,
Let nature's melody draw us near

In the gentle breeze, a dizzied trance,
Nature's canvas, a joyful dance.
Nature brings the leaves of trees green
The rain makes our hearts joyous and clean

With morning's chorus, birds unite,
Their chirps and tweets were a pure delight.
They sing of days yet to unfold,
In nature's symphony, stories untold.

Youthful spirits, in jubilant flight,
Dancing through the day and night.
With each bloom, a tale untold,
Spring's embrace is a treasure to behold.

In spring's embrace, the world awakes,
As Modar blooms by rivers' lakes.
Polash flowers paint the scene,
In shades of red, a vibrant dream.

Festivities bloom in every town,
With laughter, dance, and joy unbound.
As fields await the farmer's hand,
Spring's promise spreads across the land.

So let us dance to nature's tune,
Beneath the golden, sunlit moon.
In spring's sweet kiss, we find our bliss,
As life renews with each gentle kiss

****

(NOTE: Modar and Polash are red, flowering trees blooming during Spring)

Journey Through Nambor: Discovering Deopani's Sacred Serenity

In Nambor's embrace,
where jungles thrive,
Through winding roads
our spirits revive.

Tall trees stand sentinel,
a majestic sight,
As Dhansiri's
waters dance in delight.

Beside the path,
a haven of relief,
Hot springs bubble,
soothing our belief.

Nature's Pharmacy,
where ailments flee,
Beneath the shade of
a healing tree.

Silonijan's bounty,
fruits and greens,
A vibrant tapestry,
nature's scenes.

Handicrafts adorn
the roadside fair,
Crafted with love,
they beckon us there.

At Deopani's shrine,
ancient and revered,
Goddess Durga's grace,
forever endeared.

Lamps aglow,
prayers rise in the air,
Her blessings bestowed,
with tender care.

Within her sanctum,
hearts humbly bow,
In her presence,
serenity enshroud.

Gratitude flows,
as we depart the shrine,
In her embrace,
may all futures shine.

With each step taken,
her blessings soar,
Guiding us onward,
forevermore.

In the beauty of Nambor,
and Ma Durga's embrace,
May peace reign eternal,
in every space.

BROWNIE – MY FRIEND

In a cozy little house near town,
Lives a pup named Brownie, with a coat of brown.
With a wag of his tail and a bark so loud,
He's the goofiest dog, always drawing a crowd.

From sunrise to sunset, he's full of cheer,
Bounding through fields without fear.
Chasing his tail with endless delight,
Pouncing on squirrels with all his might.

Brownie loves treats; that's no surprise,
His nose wiggles with eager eyes.
He gobbles biscuits, bones, and more,
Leaving crumbs on carpets, treats galore.

Mischief follows Brownie wherever he goes,
Digging gardens, stealing socks from toes.
He splashes in puddles, rolls in mud,
Leaving paw prints, a mischievous flood.

Yet despite his antics, we love him so,
With boundless energy, a joyful glow.
He's our loyal companion, furry friend,
Bringing laughter and love that never ends.

Here's to Brownie, our playful pup,
With his wagging tail and goofy strut.
May his days be filled with treats and fun,
Our mischievous Brownie, our number one!

A beauty to behold

In the land where colours dance,
A maiden's beauty does entrance.
Her eyes, deep as twilight skies,
Reflect the stars, where passion lies.

Her skin, like silk, so smooth and fair,
Glistens in the sunlight's glare.
With every step, a graceful glide,
In her presence, hearts collide.

Her smile, a beacon, pure and bright,
Guides lost souls through the darkest night.
Her laughter, like a melody sweet,
Echoes through the bustling street.

In her hair, the fragrance of jasmine blooms,
A symphony of nature's perfumes.
Her voice, a melody divine,
Captivates like vintage wine.

With every glance, a story told,
Of mysteries ancient, yet untold.
In her, the beauty of a thousand moons,
A goddess among earthly dunes.

For in her, the essence of grace,
A portrait of elegance in every trace.
In the eyes of youth, she's a radiant pearl,
An Indian girl, a precious swirl.

The musical melody

In the heart of our college's bustling halls,
There walks a maiden, fair and tall.
With hair like midnight, cascading down,
And eyes like lotus, jewels in her crown.

Her skin, as smooth as porcelain's grace,
Her smile was a sunbeam on her face.
With every step, a dance so light,
Captivating all with pure delight.

Her voice, a melody sweet and pure,
Like a cuckoo's song, forever sure.
In her presence, hearts do soar,
For she's the one that we adore.

In classrooms bright, her brilliance shines,
A star amid the academic lines.
With knowledge vast and wisdom deep,
In her, secrets of the universe we seek.

But amidst the books and scholarly grace,
Lies a maiden with a radiant face.
The melody of honeyed grace
With each step she takes, a dance of gentle embrace

And amid our college days,
I found myself lost in her gaze.
For in her, I saw a beauty rare,
A soul so pure, beyond compare.

With trembling hands and hearts aflame,
I gathered the courage to speak her name.
In whispers soft, my love I professed,
Hoping she'd hear and be impressed.

And after days of longing and fear,
I finally spoke, through joy and tear.
To my surprise, she turned to me,
And with a smile, she set me free.

For in her eyes, I found my home,
A pure love, forever known.
And in her arms, I found my place,
In the embrace of her sweet embrace.

So here's to the girl with the long black hair,
The one who captured my heart, unaware.

For in her, I found my truest love,
A gift from the heavens, from above.

Ode to Our Teachers

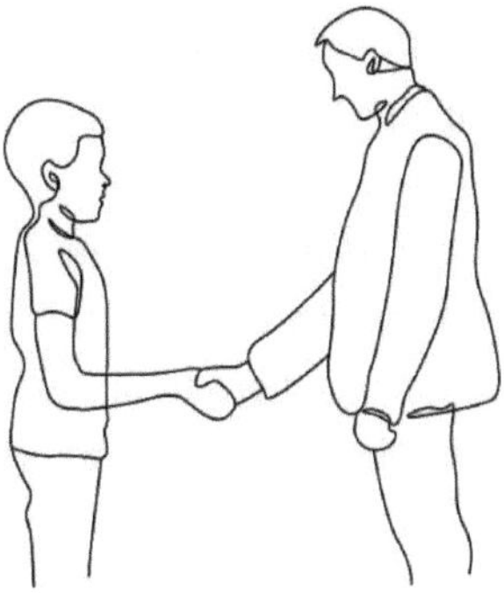

In halls where echoes softly tread,
Where dreams are taught, where hearts are led,
Our teachers stand with wisdom's grace,
In every classroom's sacred space.

With patient eyes and gentle hands,
They guide us through life's shifting sands,
With lessons drawn from hearts so wide,
In every step, our spirits guide.

They shape the mind; they stir the soul,
In every story, every goal,
With knowledge pure and wisdom deep,
They plant the dreams we hold and keep.

Through early mornings, sleepless nights,
In shadows where their courage lights,
They carve the paths where futures bloom,
In classrooms' soft, embracing room.

They saw the spark within our eyes,
In whispered hopes and silent sighs,
And nurtured dreams with tender care,
In every word, in every stare.

They taught us more than books can tell,
In every lesson, every spell,
With kindness where their spirits dwell,
They rang the dreams' awakening bell.

Their sacrifices, known but rare,
In moments where their hearts laid bare,
Reflect the love they chose to share,
In spaces where the dreams repair.

In every test, in every tear,
They stood as pillars, ever near,
With courage where our fears appear,
They held our hands and calmed our fear.

For every child they guided bright,
In shadows where they lit the light,
They shaped the world in quiet might,
In dawns where every dream takes flight.

So let us honor, let us raise,
Our voices in their endless praise,
For teachers who, through countless days,
Have shaped the paths our hearts now blaze.

In every life where hope begins,
In every heart where courage wins,
Their spirit flows, their legacy,
A beacon through eternity.

To teachers who have shown the way,
In every night, in every day,
We bow in gratitude and say,
Your love has carved the light's array.

For you have made us who we are,
In dreams you set, in guiding star,
Your wisdom shines forever far,
In hearts where true reflections are.

Bihu Bliss: A Springtime Symphony

In the land of Assam, where springtime reigns,
Bihu bells chime a joyful refrain.
Young girls sway in vibrant attire,
Boys join the dance, hearts full of fire.

Husori echoes through fields so green,
Elders and youths, a jubilant scene.
Cows and bullocks, revered with care,
Their blessings sought in the morning air.

Tractors hum, in fields they roam,
Yet tradition thrives in every home.
Paddy fields await, for hands to sow,
A promise of harvest, a bounty to grow.

Namghar stands tall in the village square,
Prayers ascend in the fragrant air.
Delicacies abound, a feast for all,
Shared with laughter at Bihu's call.

Cuckoos sing in the trees above,
Ketekis join in a symphony of love.
Bihu's rhythm beats in every heart,
A celebration of life, a vibrant art.

So let us dance, and let us sing,
To the tune of Bihu, let our spirits ring.
For in this festival, we find our connection,
To our roots, our land, in sweet affection.

(BIHU in Assam, a state of India, is the main festival celebrated in April)

Autumn's Embrace

Under autumn's golden leaves, we stand,
Years etched in lines upon our hands,
A lifetime of love, joy, and grace,
Reflected in your gentle face.

The world has turned, seasons changed,
Yet our hearts remain unchained,
Through the winters, springs, and summers
gone,
Our love's enduring as the dawn.

We've faced the days, both dark and bright,
Together, love's guiding light,
Through every challenge, joy, and tear,
Our hearts have grown, year by year.

Your touch, a comfort in the cold,
A story of love in whispers told,
In every wrinkle, a tale of time,
In every heartbeat, a tender rhyme.

The leaves fall in their amber dance,
We sway in love's eternal trance,
Memories of youth and dreams we shared,
Now aged with wisdom, gently paired.

In the autumn breeze, our whispers blend,
Promises kept, and wounds we mend,
The beauty of a love so true,
In your eyes, the world renewed.

We walk beneath the fading sky,
Hand in hand, hearts awry,
In each step, a lifetime's song,
Where we belong, all along.

As twilight casts its golden hue,
I see my past and future too,
In the embrace of autumn’s kiss,
We find a love that's pure bliss.

In this season, our hearts align,
Timeless echoes, intertwine,
Two souls in love's endless dance,
In autumn's glow, our love enchants.

Through the rustling leaves, we hear,
The echoes of each passing year,
In every rustle, every sigh,
We find our love under the sky.

As stars emerge in evening’s grace,
We stand, enduring love's embrace,
In this moment, pure and tender,
Our hearts will always remember.

Lotus in the Moonlight

In the garden where moonlight weaves,
There stands a beauty who quietly grieves,
Her hair, a cascade of midnight's glow,
Adorned with a lotus, soft and slow.

Her long black tresses, flowing like silk,
Shimmer in the moon's gentle ilk,
Each strand a tale of endless night,
Glistening with the stars' soft light.

Her eyes, deep as a tranquil lake,
Reflect wisdom, dreams awake,
Intelligent orbs that silently speak,
Of love profound and passions meek.

With a shy smile, she softly glows,
A blush that only the moonlight knows,
Her heart, a secret, tender, and true,
Unveiled in moments, precious and few.

Her giggles, a melody, light and clear,
Echo-like chimes that all can hear,
Infectious joy that softly spreads,
Like ripples in a moonlit thread.

She moves with grace, a rhythmic sway,
In sarees that dance in night's soft play,
Each step a whisper, a gentle song,
A dance that carries the night along.

The saree wraps her in colors bright,
A silhouette bathed in ethereal light,
Golden threads and crimson hues,
Weaving a tapestry of dusk's soft views.

Her presence, a blend of earth and sky,
A lotus in the moonlight's sigh,
In every gesture, a tale unfolds,
Of beauty rare and grace untold.

With every step, her rhythm flows,
Like river's dance where moonlight glows,
Her saree, a canvas, night adorned,
A portrait of elegance, gently born.

In the hush of the night, she blooms,
A lotus kissed by silver moon,
Her beauty, a serene, timeless grace,
Reflected in her moonlit face.

Her walk, a symphony in the night,
A dance of shadows, pure delight,
In sarees that flow with whispered song,
She carries the beauty of dreams along.

As stars look down, the heavens sigh,
Enchanted by her, as am I,
For in her grace, the world does see,
The lotus, a symbol of pure beauty.

Retirement Rhythms: A Poetic Journey

In the realm of retirement, a tale so often told,
Of a once vital figure, now feeling quite old.
His wisdom once sought, his advice held so dear,
Now finds himself lonely, with nobody near.

People once clamored for his sage point of view,
Now they're off on their own, bid him adieu.
He's become like old furniture, left in the dust,
His relevance waning, his spirit's now crushed.

His spouse, once enamored, now gives him the slip,
Preferring her own company to his verbal quip.
His kids, they've flown off, chasing their dreams,
Leaving poor dad to ponder, or so it seems.

He tries to engage, to keep boredom at bay,
But alas, his attempts are met with dismay.
For who wants to listen to tales of the past?
When the present moves on, oh, so fast!

So he sits in his chair, with a sigh and a groan,
Feeling more like a statue than a flesh-and-bone.
His jokes fall flat, his stories grow stale,
Oh, retirement's a ship with a leaky old sail.

But fear not, dear retiree, there's still hope in sight,
For laughter can conquer even the darkest night.
So embrace your new role with humor and cheer,
And remember, old age is just another frontier!

The Dance of Desire

In dawn's soft light, where whispers wake,
She walks, a muse, the heavens make.
Her eyes, twin stars in velvet skies,
Shine with a spark that never dies.

Mischief dances in her gaze,
A twinkle where the moonlight plays.
Bright, intelligent, wild, and free,
They hold a world of mystery.

Her hair, a midnight river flows,
With jasmine blooms, where passion grows.
Long, flowing, black, a silken stream,
That weaves through twilight's gentle dream.

It drapes her pointed breasts with grace,
A veil that shadows her embrace.
Each toss of hair, a playful dare,
Yet always, it returns to care.

Her skin, like bronze in softest glow,
A canvas kissed by dawn's first show.
Each curve, each line, a tender grace,
A warm caress in time and space.

Her lips, a ruby's secret hue,
Where whispers deep of love ensue.
They part in laughter, soft and bright,
A smile that warms the coldest night.

Her neck, a sculpted arch of light,
Where shadows blend in soft twilight.
The hollow there, a tender sigh,
Where silent dreams and secrets lie.

Her breasts, like gentle hills that rise,
Beneath the stars and moonlit skies.
Each curve a soft, inviting line,
Where lovers' hearts and dreams entwine.

Her waist, a slender, graceful arc,
A gentle line in evening's dark.
Each touch, each glance, a lover's path,
A journey in her warm embrace.

Her hips, they sway in gentle dance,
A rhythm where desires prance.
They move in tender, fluid song,
Where earth and sky in love belong.

Her legs, like pillars in the breeze,
They stride with elegance and ease.
Each step, a kiss upon the ground
Where sensual dreams and hearts are found.

Her feet, they tread on earth so light,
With every move, a touch of night.
She walks, a melody of grace,
A symphony, a warm embrace.

Her sari, draped in hues divine,
A whisper soft in twilight's shine.
Each fold a story, gently pressed,
Against the curves where dreams caressed.

Her scent, a jasmine's tender breath,
Invades the senses, weaves through depth.
A fragrance rich, a lover's dream,
In every touch, in every gleam.

Her voice, a velvet murmur low,
A caress that sets the heart aglow.
It lingers in the morning air,
A song of love, so sweet and rare.

Her glance, a warmth that softly burns,
In every look, a heart returns.
For in her eyes, her touch, her smile,
The world finds love, and time's beguiled.

She moves, a symphony so sweet,
A dance where earth and heavens meet.
In every step, a story spun,
Of love, of life, of hearts as one.

She is a vision, pure and kind,
A dream of warmth, a tender mind.
In every breath, in every gleam,
She paints the world's most vivid dream.

A victory song

In the heart of adversity,
a challenge was born,
With scant resources,
we faced the storm.

The management's decree,
a mountain to climb,
Yet with a dedicated team,
we embraced the time.

Through trials and tribulation
we pressed on
Each obstacle conquered
Each doubt withdrawn.

With grit and determination,
we forged ahead,
In the face of adversity,
we were not misled.

The task was daunting,
the journey long,
But together we stood,
united and strong.

With sweat on our brows and
fire in our hearts,
We tackled the challenge,
playing our parts.

No accolade or trophy
could match the thrill,
Of overcoming odds,
with sheer force of will.

For the impact on society,
we strive to impart,
A legacy of perseverance,
etched in our hearts.

With joy unbounded,
we celebrate the feat,
A testament to teamwork,
victory sweet.

For in the face of adversity,
we found our way,
And in triumph, we stand,
come what may.

So here's to the journey,
the struggles we've known,
For in overcoming,
true greatness is shown.

Let the world
take note of our triumph song,
For together,
we've proved, we truly belong.

An evening on the Sandy shore

In twilight's embrace,
by the sandy shore,
Where the sun meets the sea,
the heavens explore.
A canvas painted with hues divine,
As day bids farewell, and stars align.

Golden rays
dance upon the waves,
A symphony of light,
nature craves.
Reflecting on the water's sheen,
A mirror of beauty, serene.

The tide whispers
secrets to the sand,
As it caresses
the earth's gentle hand.
With each gentle kiss,
a story unfolds,
Of ancient tales,
and myths untold.

Seagulls glide
on the ocean's breath,
Their cries harmonize
with nature's depth.
A melody of freedom,
in flight they soar,
Above the waves'
eternal roar.

As darkness descends,
the moon takes flight,
Casting its glow
upon the night.
Silver beams cascade,
a celestial display,
Guiding souls
on their nocturnal way.

Lifeguards stand vigilant,
guardians of the night,
Guiding wanderers
from danger's sight.
Their watchful eyes,
a beacon of hope,
In the vast expanse,
where dreams elope.

Beneath the stars,
the world's at peace,
A moment of stillness,
where worries cease.
In this tranquil haven,
where land meets sea,
The beauty of nature
sets spirits free.

So let us linger
in this twilight's embrace,
And cherish the beauty
of this sacred place.
For in the dance of sun and sea,
find the essence of tranquility
for you and me.

Triumph in the wilderness

In the heart of the wilderness, where silence roared,
A daunting task before us, no easy road explored.
With no means to reach beyond our sight,
We faced the challenge, prepared to fight.

Instead of despair, we saw a chance,
To take a leap, to make a stance.
A dedicated team, brave and true,
Together as one, we'd see it through.

Through rugged paths and skies so gray,
We forged ahead, day by day.
Every stone, every tree, a test to meet,
With hearts on fire, no thought of defeat.

In unity, we found our strength,
Pushed past limits, went the length.
Through sweat and toil, with hands so firm,
We built a dream from earth and germ.

Laughter echoed in the nights so cold,
Stories of courage, bold and old.
In every sunrise, hope anew,
With every sunset, our spirits grew.

No trophy's needed, no golden prize,
Could match the light in our own eyes.
The joy we felt, the bonds we made,
A spontaneous heart's parade.

When at last the task was done,
We stood together; we had won.
Not just a challenge, but a memory grand,
In the heart of that untamed land.

We danced and sang beneath the stars,
Forgotten were the wounds and scars.
A celebration pure, a victory bright,
In the silent embrace of the night.

For in the end, the greatest feat,
Is not the goal, but hearts that beat.
With shared dreams and hands held tight,
We turned the dark into light.

No award or reward could ever compare,
To the heartfelt joy, we all did share.
For in that wilderness, so wild and free,
We found our truest victory.

So here's to the challenge, the team, the drive,
The spirit that kept us all alive.
In tough terrain, we made our mark,
A journey of souls, igniting the dark

A Journey of Hearts

In a quiet home, a mother stays,
Her heart is torn in many ways.
Her son's now grown, a father too,
With twins so sweet, her world anew.

Her daughter calls from lands afar,
A longing voice, a distant star.
"Come visit, Mom, and stay awhile,
I miss your laugh, I miss your smile."

Her heart is torn, her mind adrift,
In her chest, a heavy rift.
She loves her grands, their joy, their cheer,
But misses her daughter, ever dear.

The days are filled with tiny feet,
Laughter ringing, moments sweet.
But at night, her mind does stray,
To foreign lands, so far away.

Her daughter knew the weight she bore,
Came home to open a new door.
"Mom, come with me, just for a spell,
There's so much more I'd like to tell."

She couldn't say no, though heart was torn,
To leave her loves, the morn to morn.
With a heavy sigh and a hopeful heart,
She packed her bags, a brand new start.

The plane took off, her thoughts entwined,
Excitement mixed with fear combined.
A new routine, a different way,
A foreign land, a brighter day.

The culture new, the language strange,
Her mind adrift in endless change.
But through it all, her daughter's hand,
Guiding her through this unknown land.

She missed the twins, their joyous cries,
The sparkle in their tiny eyes.
But here she found a different grace,
In her daughter's love, a warm embrace.

Her friend had said to seize the day,
"Enjoy the journey, come what may."
And so she did, though heartstrings pulled,
In this new life, her spirit fueled.

She learned to love the foreign streets,
The different tastes, the varied beats.
Yet always in her heart did stay,
Her grandkids' smiles, not far away.

In time, she found a peace within,
A balance in the lives she'd spin.
The bonds of love, they stretch and bend,
But never truly reach an end.

Returning home, her heart was light,
With memories of days so bright.
She knew now, love's a journey too,
With every step, a bond renews.

For though the miles may come between,
And life may shift, unseen, serene,
The ties of love remain unbroken,
In every word, in every token.

Joyful Heart

In the heart of an Indian village,
where rivers gently flow,
Lives Meera, her hair free
and black as night's glow.

It dances in the evening light,
a captivating sea,
A cascade of curls,
flowing wild and free.

Her hair framed her face so well,
cascaded down her back,
In playful curls and silken swirls,
like the evening sky turned black.

When breezes blew, it danced with grace,
caressed her rosy cheek,
A mesmerizing spectacle,
that left the boys so weak.

Her eyes, deep pools of mystery,
dark and full of dreams,
They sparkled with hidden fire,
like stars' celestial beams.

At every glance, a story told,
of mischief, joy, and light
Her smile, a beacon bright
and warm, in the softest twilight.

She walked with enchanting grace,
her anklets softly chimed,
Each step, a melody of life,
in perfect rhythm timed.

In festivals, she led the dance,
her laughter filled the air,
With every twirl, her hair would swirl,
like poetry laid bare.

Her voice, a song of happiness,
so jolly, sweet, and pure,
Echoed through village lanes,
a melody to adore.

She joined in every festivity,
her spirit wild and free,
A lotus blooming in the sun,
beneath the banyan tree.

Among the crowd, a boy named Arjun,
watched her from afar,
With dreams of holding her hand
Beneath the evening star.

He was tall, with eyes of brown and hair of
chestnut hue,
A smile that shone with innocence, his heart so
strong and true.

One day, by the riverside,
where lotuses do bloom,
Their paths did cross, their worlds aligned,
dispelling all the gloom.

Meera, with her joyous heart, and Arjun,
shy but kind,
In shared smiles and stolen glances,
a bond began to bind.

They met beneath the mango tree,
where blossoms scented sweet,
With every laugh and gentle word,
their hearts began to beat.

Arjun praised her flowing hair, her eyes that
sparkled bright,
Meera blushed a rosy red beneath the soft
moonlight.

Their friendship grew in moments small,
in laughter and in tears,
Through every monsoon rain, they walked,
dispelling all their fears.

In fields of green, by temple bells,
their love began to grow,
With every whispered secret shared,
their souls began to glow.

One festival of lights arrived,
with lamps that shone so clear,
Arjun took her hand in his,
and whispered in her ear,

"Meera, you're the brightest star,
in my ever-darkened night,
With you, my heart finds solace,
my world feels ever bright."

She smiled, her eyes a twinkling, her hair a
silken veil,
In that moment, love was born, a wondrous,
sacred tale.

They danced beneath the stars that night, in
rhythms soft and sweet,
In every step, in every touch, their hearts found a
steady beat.

Through seasons changing, love remained,
a constant in their lives,
In fields of gold, in winter's chill, their bond
ever thrives.

From playful teens to lovers true, they grew in
tender grace,
In the heart of an Indian village, their love found
a perfect place.

So here's to Meera, with her hair, as dark as
midnight's shade,
And Arjun, with his earnest heart, in love's
sweet serenade.

For in the dance of youthful love, beneath the
stars above,
We find the magic, pure and true, of first and
lasting love.

The Radiance of Time

In twilight where the day moves slow,
And evening's colors softly flow,
She sits, aglow where breezes blow,
A beauty, time now lets us know.

Her hair, now silver, gently shines,
Threads where moonlight quietly dines,
A crown of years, where wisdom aligns,
In echoes where true grace refines.

Her eyes, though aged, still sparkle bright,
With warmth and joy, a soft delight,
In every gaze, a world of light,
A beacon in the calm of night.

Her skin, with lines where stories live,
In every touch, warmth she can give,
A map of life, where joys forgive,
In wrinkles where her smiles revive.

She moves with grace, though time has passed,
In every step, a dance that's cast,
A gentle rhythm, slow and vast,
In moments where her spirit's fast.

Her laughter, like a song so clear,
A melody that all hearts hear,
In every note, a joy sincere,
A comfort where all worries clear.

Her hands, though worn, still softly hold,
A tenderness that's pure and bold,
In every touch, a warmth of gold,
In hearts where love and joy unfold.

Her smile, a dawn in twilight's rest,
A light within her gentle jest,
In every curve, a love expressed,
A joy that's timeless, well confessed.

Her presence, like a summer's day,
In every word, a warm display,
A glow that never fades away,
A light where all the sorrows sway.

Through years where life has gently spun,
In moments where true hearts are won,
Her beauty shines as bright as sun,
In twilight where true joys are spun

So let her joy and beauty bloom,
In every smile that clears the gloom,
A radiant light in twilight's room,
A beauty where true hearts resume.

The Garden of Her Joy

In gardens where the flowers fade,
Where twilight dances in soft shade,
She stands, a bloom where joys cascade
A beauty time has gently made.

Her hair, a soft and silver hue,
Falls like dew in morning's view,
A crown where age and grace renew,
A touch where tender breezes blew.

Her eyes, a mirror of the skies,
Reflect the dawn where laughter flies,
At every glance, a joy implies,
A world where simple beauty lies.

Her skin, with tales that time does weave,
In every line, a past to leave,
4A map of life, where hearts believe,
In wrinkles where her love does cleave.

She moves with grace, a gentle dance,
In every step, a life's romance,
A rhythm where true joys enhance,
In moments where her heart's expanse.

Her laughter, like a brook's sweet song,
A melody that flows along,
In every note, where hearts belong,
A tune where true delights prolong.

Her hands, though aged, still tenderly,
Hold the world with love's decree,
In every touch, where hearts agree,
A warmth where love and joy run free.

Her smile, a sunrise softly traced,
A glow within the twilight's taste,
In every curve, where hearts embraced,
A light that no time can erase.

Her presence, like a gentle breeze,
In whispers where the heart finds ease,
A symphony where spirits please,
A melody that never flees.

In every bloom, in every seed,
In moments where the heart does lead,
Her beauty grows in time's true creed,
A garden where true joys proceed.

So let her grace and joy be known,
In every heart where love is shown,
A beauty where true hearts have grown,
A garden where her light is sown.

The Tapestry of Her Grace

In the evening where stars ignite,
Where twilight falls in tender light,
She weaves her grace, both soft and bright,
A beauty time has etched in sight.

Her hair, now silver, softly flows,
Threads where twilight gently glows,
A crown where life's own wisdom grows,
In whispers where the evening blows.

Her eyes, though marked by years gone by,
Still hold a sparkle, soft and shy,
In every glance, a gentle sigh,
A warmth where love and memories lie.

Her skin, a canvas of her life,
With lines that tell of joy and strife,
In every touch, a love that's rife,
A tapestry of days and nights.

She moves with grace, though slower now,
In every step, a gentle vow,
A rhythm where true joys endow,
A dance where hearts in love avow.

Her laughter, like a soft refrain,
A melody that soothes all pain,
In every note, a gentle gain,
A song that falls like gentle rain.

Her hands, though worn by time's embrace,
Still hold with love, a gentle trace,
In every touch, a warmest grace,
A comfort in her soft embrace.

Her smile, a dawn in evening's veil,
A light within her joyful tale,
In every curve, where hearts unveil,
A joy that's steady, never frail.

Her presence, like a summer breeze,
In whispers where the heart finds ease,
A symphony that softly frees,
A melody that never flees.

In every thread of life's long weave,
In moments where the heart does grieve,
Her beauty shines in time's reprieve,
A tapestry where love believes.

So let her joy and beauty stand,
In every heart, in every hand,
A radiance where life is grand,
A tapestry of love so planned.

The Splendor of Brahmaputra's Embrace

In Brahmaputra's flowing grace,
Where waters glide in calm embrace,
The river's magic finds its place,
As dreams take shape and softly trace.

The Brahmaputra, grand and wide,
Flows through Assam with quiet pride,
In currents where the earth's tied,
A lifeline carved and gently applied.

Its waters, silver threads that gleam,
Reflect the sky's soft morning beam,
In ripples where the daylight's stream
Unfolds each wonder like a dream.

The cruise begins, a quiet delight,
Through Brahmaputra's soft twilight,
In mornings where the dawn's first light
Turns every view to pure delight.

On deck, the breezes softly play,
Through whispering reeds and shadows' sway,
In every wave where reflections lay,
A melody of a bright new day.

The shores with villages in view,
Where life is touched by morning's hue,
In scenes both bright and calm and true,
A tapestry where day is new.

The green hills rise, the forests stand,
At every glance, a fresh command,
In Brahmaputra's loving hand,
A beauty where the heart expands.

The islands, breathing with the tide,
In sands where peaceful whispers bide,
A sanctuary set aside,
In moments where true peace resides.

As twilight falls and stars appear,
In skies where night draws ever near,
The river glows, dreams revere,
In waters where the heart is clear.

The cruise through Brahmaputra's grace,
Each ripple holds a time and place,
A journey through an endless space,
Where heart and river interlace.

So let the river's song resound,
In Brahmaputra's flowing ground,
A symphony where joys are found,
In currents where true hearts are bound.

Brahmaputra's Gentle Serenade

In Brahmaputra's gentle glide,
Where waters flow both deep and wide,
A river cruise becomes our guide,
Through beauty where calm dreams reside.

The Brahmaputra's vast expanse,
In every wave and every glance,
Reflects the sun's soft golden dance,
In rhythms where true joys enhance.

Its waters, mirrors of the sky,
Hold clouds and birds as they pass by,
In currents where dawn's light does lie,
Each day begins with tender sigh.

The cruise, a vessel in delight,
Moves gently through the morning light,
On journeys where the heart takes flight,
Through sceneries both calm and bright.

On deck, where breezes softly play,
Through reeds where whispers softly sway,
The river's song begins its lay,
A melody of a perfect day.

The shores with forests lush and green,
Where life in quiet breath is seen,
In every scene where rivers lean,
A harmony of twilight's sheen.

The islands, resting soft and fair,
In Brahmaputra's gentle care,
A paradise where silence shares,
Its beauty in the twilight's stare.

The mountains rise with distant views,
In shadows where the night renews,
The Brahmaputra's gentle clues,
Of mysteries where dreams pursue.

As night descends and stars now gleam,
In waters where reflections dream,
The river's glow, a tender theme,
A journey through a timeless stream.

The cruise, a passage through the night,
In Brahmaputra's soothing light,
In every ripple, pure and bright,
A voyage through the heart's own sight.

So let the river's beauty flow,
In Brahmaputra's gentle glow,
A serenade where hearts can grow,
In peace, where dreams and waters know.

The Enchantment of Brahmaputra's Path

In Brahmaputra's gentle sway,
Where waters guide the heart's own way,
A river cruise begins to play,
A journey through the light of day.

The Brahmaputra, strong and wide,
Flows through the land with endless pride,
In currents where the dreams reside,
A lifeline where true wonders bide.

Its waters, like a painter's touch,
Reflect the sky where colors blush,
In every wave, a tender hush,
Where beauty flows in nature's rush.

The cruise, a vessel on its course,
Glides through the river's gentle force,
In pathways where the heart's resource
Finds peace in Brahmaputra's source.

On deck, where breezes softly sweep,
Through reeds where silent whispers creep,
In every wave where stories sleep,
A melody where dreams do leap.

The shores, where forests bend and grow,
In vistas where the rivers flow,
Hold tales where life and nature show
Scenes where beauty's endless glow.

The islands, where the river's grace,
Finds sanctuary in a tranquil place,
In Brahmaputra's warm embrace,
A haven where true joys find space.

As twilight falls in gentle shade,
In skies where night and day parade,
The river's glow begins to fade,
In Brahmaputra's serenade.

The cruise, a passage through the dusk,
In Brahmaputra's gentle musk,
In every wave where moments bask,
A journey where the heart does trust.

So let the river's tale unfold,
In Brahmaputra's flowing gold,
A story where the heart is bold,
In waters where true dreams are told.

The river flows in endless streams,
In Brahmaputra's gentle beams,
A voyage through the heart's own dreams,
In currents where pure beauty gleams.

The Dichotomy of Light and Shadow

In twilight's gentle, fleeting glow,
Where shadows weave and moonbeams flow,
A dance unfolds, both soft and slow,
The tale of light and shadow shows.

In the morning's birth, the light expands,
Across the skies, o'er seas, and lands,
It touches all with golden hands,
Dispelling night's dark, mystic strands.

Yet shadows linger, soft and deep,
In forest glades, where secrets sleep,
In valleys where the echoes keep,
The whispers where the shadows weep.

Light reveals the world's bright face,
In every dawn, in every grace,
But shadows, in their silent space,
Define the lines, the hidden trace.

The light is truth; it clears the haze,
It warms the heart, it guides the gaze,
But shadows, in their quiet ways,
Hold mysteries the light displays.

In sunlight's beam, the truth is bared,
In shadow's cloak, the fears are spared,
Together, they are always paired,
In contrast, where the beauty is shared.

A life of light, a world too bright,
Would blind the eyes, would scorch the sight,
Yet endless shadow, endless night,
Would drown the soul, obscure the flight.

Their dance, a balance finely spun,
In every dusk, in every sun,
Reveals a world where both are one,
In harmony, their tale is done.

So in the heart, both light and shade,
In every joy, in every fade,
Are threads in life's grand tapestry made,
Where beauty blooms in both displayed.

For light and shadow, intertwined,
Create a world where hearts can find,
A depth of truth and peace combined,
In shadows where the light is lined.

In twilight's gleam, in dawn's embrace,
In every line on every face,
The dance of light and shadow's grace,
Is where we find our true, shared space.

Reflections of the Human Soul

In the quiet of morning, as the world wakes,
We wander through thoughts, through feelings,
Seeking meaning in the ordinary,
A simple touch, a fleeting glance.

Our lives, a mosaic of moments,
Fragments of joy, shards of sorrow,
Each piece tells a story,
Of who we are, of who we hope to be.

Beneath our skin, deeper than flesh,
Lies the essence of our being,
A soul woven with dreams and fears,
With love that defies logic and reason.

We reach for the stars, for the infinite,
Yet our feet remain grounded in the now,
In the laughter of friends, the warmth of family,
In the struggles and triumphs of every day.

In every smile, a universe resides,
In every tear, a world of pain,
We are the sum of our experiences,
A tapestry of the seen and the unseen.

We seek connection, a touch, a word,
A reminder that we are not alone,
In this vast, chaotic dance of existence,
We find solace in each other's presence.

Our hearts beat in rhythm with the world,
In sync with the tides, the seasons,
We are nature; we are nurtured,
A blend of the tangible and the ethereal.

In the silence of the night, we ponder,
The mysteries of our hearts and minds,
The paradoxes of love and loss,
The beauty in the broken and the whole.

We are stories in motion, ever unfolding,
Chapters written with each breath,
A dance of light and shadow,
Of knowing and unknowing.

In the mirror, we see ourselves,
Not just flesh, but spirit,
A reflection of the infinite,
In the eyes of the finite.

For in the simplicity of our days,
Lies the profound, the complex,
The essence of what it means to be human,
To love, to hurt, to hope, to dream.

We are the whispers of the universe,
The echoes of ancient truths,
Living, breathing, feeling,
In the endless journey of the soul.

Echoes of the Sublime

In the maze of consciousness, we tread lightly,
Navigating the corridors of thought and feeling,
Where shadows dance with fleeting light,
And whispers of the sublime caress our souls.

Our existence, a paradox of the infinite and the finite,
Embodied in the ephemeral beauty of a moment,
A transient breath in the continuum of time,
Yet holding within it the echoes of eternity.

We traverse the landscape of the mind,
A terrain both familiar and enigmatic,
Where memories bloom like forgotten flowers,
And dreams weave tapestries of possibility.

In the stillness of contemplation, we encounter the profound,
The ineffable truths that lie beneath the surface,
The silent symphony of the cosmos,
Resonating within the depths of our being.

Our hearts, vessels of boundless capacity,
Hold the weight of love and loss,
Of joy that transcends the mundane,

And the sorrow that carves the contours of our humanity.

We seek understanding in the abstract,
Grasping at the intangible threads of meaning,
In the interstices of reality and perception,
Where the known dissolves into the unknown.

In the dance of relationships, we find our reflection,
Mirrored in the eyes of others,
A complex interplay of connection and isolation,
Of unity and divergence.

The essence of our existence lies in the paradox,
Of seeking permanence in a transient world,
Of finding clarity amid chaos,
Of embracing the finite while yearning for the infinite.

Our journey is a dialogue with the universe,
A conversation of silence and sound,
Of presence and absence,
Of light and shadow.

We are the architects of our narrative,
Crafting stories from the fragments of experience,
Building meaning from the ruins of the past,

And the dreams of the future.

In the quiet moments of introspection,
We touch the edges of the ineffable,
Glimpsing the vastness within and without,
The boundless horizons of the soul.

Our lives, a canvas of contradictions,
Painted with the hues of emotion,
The interplay of existence,
Where light and dark coalesce.

In the pursuit of wisdom, we encounter humility,
The realization of our limitations,
The recognition of the vastness beyond our grasp,
Yet the relentless drive to seek to understand.

We are the sum of our experiences,
A mosaic of the seen and the unseen,
The spoken and the unspoken,
The lived and the imagined.

In the embrace of the present, we find eternity,
In the fleeting moments, the timeless,
In the ephemeral, the everlasting,
In the mundane, the miraculous.

Our journey, an odyssey of the heart and mind,
Navigating the currents of existence,
Guided by the stars of hope and memory,
Towards the infinite horizon of our potential.

For in the essence of our humanity,
Lies the reflection of the divine,
The whispers of the cosmos,
Echoing within the chambers of our soul.

We are the bearers of light in the darkness,
The seekers of truth amid ambiguity,
The dreamers of the impossible,
The architects of the future.

In the maze of consciousness, we find our way,
Through the corridors of thought and feeling,
Guided by the echoes of the sublime,
Towards the boundless expanse of our existence.

The Enchanting Beauty of the Himalayas

The Sacred Peaks

In lands where mountains touch the sky,
The Himalayas rise on high.
Where sacred rivers start their flow,
Kedarnath's twilight whispers glow.

A temple cradled in the snow,
With tales of faith from long ago,
It stands where pure devotion grows,
Where only true believers go.

Badrinath sings the Ganges' song,
Among the peaks where rivers throng.
The temple's grace, timeless and strong,
In every heart, it does belong.

Amarnath's cavern, grand and wide,
Where Shiva's form by ice does bide.
In summer's light, where pilgrims guide,
Their hearts find faith in sacred stride.

Vaishno Devi, proud and bright,
Calls to the faithful in pure light.
Through nature's trails, their hearts ignite,
To peaks where spirits reach their height.

Rivers born from ice and snow,
Through valleys pure, they softly go.
In Rishikesh, where waters flow,
The soul in peace begins to grow.

Waterfalls in cascades break,
Each drop a dance where echoes wake.
In Tawang's rise, where prayers make
A haven where true spirits ache.

In every peak and valley deep,
The Himalayas hold and keep,
A sacred story where hearts leap,
In devotion pure and steep.

Homage to the Brave Soldiers

The Sentinel's Sacrifice

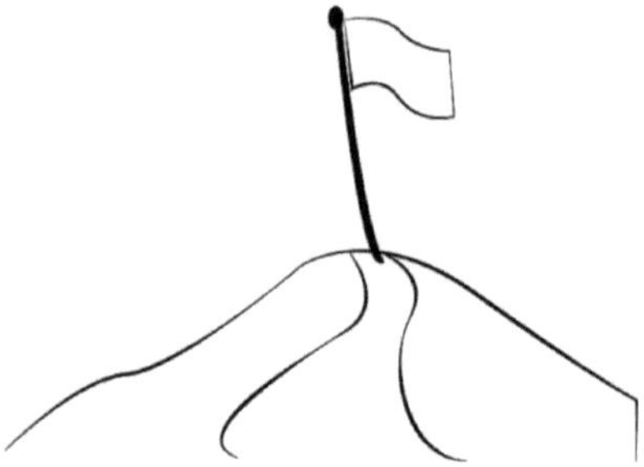

In Siachen's icy, silent night,
Where snow and stars share their light,
Our soldiers stand with iron sight,
Guarding where freedom holds tight.

On frozen ground, where eagles soar,
In winds that howl and glaciers roar,
They hold the line forevermore,
A shield where peace and justice pour.

In Arunachal's mountains high,
They stand, a beacon in the sky,
Protecting home, where spirits lie,
With steadfast faces, hearts comply.

Far from families' loving grace,
In silence where their spirits trace,
They bear their duty in this place,
A sacrifice in faith's embrace.

On battlefields where echoes blend,
In trenches where the shadows bend,
Their bravery knows no end,
In stories where true hearts ascend.

Each step on icy paths they tread,
Each night beneath the sky's dark spread,
A testament where souls have bled,
In fields where heroes' hearts are led.

Guardians brave in day and night,
On borders where their hearts are bright,
Protecting lands with honor's light,
In spirits where their courage's right.

Returning home, where peace should lay,
They find the world in disarray,
Where chaos brings their hearts to fray,
In shadows where their dreams decay.

Yet still they stand, through night and day,
In borders where their brave hearts sway,
Protecting lands where children play,
In honor where their spirits stay.

Let their sacrifice be known,
In every heart, in every home,
A legacy where freedom's grown,
In lands where honor's light has shone

The Silent Guardian

In Siachen's snow, where silence reigns,
Where icy winds and shadows wane,
Our soldiers stand, through cold and strain,
A sentinel where courage's flame.

Among the peaks where eagles soar,
In fields where shadows growl and roar,
They guard the line forevermore,
A bastion strong on freedom's core.

In Arunachal's twilight bands,
Where rivers weave through mountain lands,
They hold their duty in their hands,
On paths where honor firmly stands.

Their lives, a tale of gallant grace,
In every step, in every place,
Where duty meets the morning's face,
A legacy that hearts embrace.

Far from homes where love should bloom,
In lands where silence veils the moon,
They bear the weight of duty's loom,
In fields where shadows softly croon.

In battle's midst, where echoes rise,
In trenches where brave courage flies,
Their valor shines where danger lies,
A flame where freedom's heart relies.

Each step in snow, a sacred vow,
Each breath in cold, where dreams endow,
A testament of valor now,
In fields where honor bends to bow.

They stand as guardians, firm and bright,
In borders where the heart's own light,
Protect the lands through day and night,
A beacon through the darkest flight.

When home they come, where peace should reign,
In lands where freedom's voice should gain,
They face a world in deep disdain,
A chaos where their hearts feel pain.

Corruption's thread runs shadows deep,
In halls where justice falls asleep,
Where middlemen in darkness creep,
And ethics drown where greed does sweep.

The weak oppressed, the truth obscure,
In seas where honesty's unsure,
Where honor fails to find a cure,
In shadows where the hearts impure.

The soldier's heart, though torn and worn,
Seeks hope where justice should adorn,
In echoes where new dreams are born,
A light where freedom's heart's forlorn.

Yet still they stand through cold and storm,
In borders where their hearts stay warm,
Protecting lands where peace should form,
In honor where their spirits swarm.

In gratitude, the nation bows,
To soldiers brave, whose hearts endow,
In every step, in every vow,
A legacy where freedom plows.

So let their sacrifice be known,
In every heart, in every stone,
A beacon where true spirits own,
The lands where bravery has grown.

The Rich Diversity of the Northeast INDIA

In the Northeast, a land so pure,
With traditions rich and culture's allure,
Sattriya dance from Assam's heart,
A classical form, a divine art.

Manipuri's grace, with elegance,
Dancing tales of devotion and romance,
The gamocha, a symbol of respect,
Worn with pride, a heritage decked.

Namghars echo with prayer and song,
Where communities gather, bonds so strong,
The Hornbill Festival, Nagaland's pride,
Showcasing heritage far and wide.

Naga traditions, ancient and grand,
Warrior dances, hand in hand,
Mizo customs, vibrant and bright,
Cheraw dance, a bamboo delight.

In Arunachal's hills, traditions thrive,
Festivals of harvest, joy alive,
Manipur's rich culture, from polo's birth,
To classical dance, of unmatched worth.

The flora and fauna, a living treasure,
Rivers and forests, nature’s pleasure,
From Kaziranga’s rhinos, rare and bold,
To orchids in bloom, a sight to behold.

In Meghalaya, living root bridges stand,
Testament to harmony with the land,
Mighty Brahmaputra, lifeblood and vein,
In its vast basin, cultures remain.

Through history’s trials, we’ve stood as one,
In peace and strife, under the sun,
Our heritage, a timeless lore,
In India’s heart, forevermore.

The Allure of the Forbidden

In shadows where the daylight fades,
Where moonlight weaves through silent glades,
Two hearts find paths where longing wades,
In whispers where desire cascades.

A fleeting glance, a secret smile,
In corridors where passions pile,
The pull of something new, a while,
In spaces where the spirits beguile.

The comfort of a love grown old,
With tender touch and stories told,
Now haunted by a dream so bold,
In echoes where the shadows fold.

A touch, a breath, a word unmeant,
In stolen moments, hearts unbent,
A dance where every move is lent,
In places where the nights are spent.

In eyes where secrets softly lie,
In whispers where the shadows sigh,
Two hearts entwine beneath the sky,
In places where the dreams defy.

The thrill of something out of bounds,
In silences where truth confounds,
In every heartbeat, every sound,
A longing where the love rebounds.

Yet in the morn where daylight breaks,
Where conscience whispers, hearts awake,
The truth in every shadow shakes,
In dreams where only silence takes.

The path of fire and fleeting touch,
Where hearts betray the love so much,
In moments where the whispers clutch,
In shadows where the spirits touch.

A love that's torn by secret flames,
On nights where passion softly claims,
The heart in shadows, never tamed,
In echoes where desire frames.

In every stolen glance and breath,
In places where the shadows rest,
The truth in every whispered test,
In echoes where the heart's confessed.

So let the fire of longing burn,
In shadows where the hearts return,
In every secret, every turn,
A lesson where true hearts discern.

The Cost of Progress

The Race to Nowhere

In cities where the towers rise,
Where progress touches the skies,
People run, with weary eyes,
Chasing dreams where shadows lie.

In offices where time is sold,
Where hearts grow weary, minds grow cold,
The hours pass, the stories told,
In spaces where the dreams unfold.

Children left to play alone,
In houses where the silence's grown,
Parents' voices, a distant tone,
In echoes where the shadows moan.

In schools where pressures start to build,
Where dreams are taught, where hearts are
stilled,
The innocence of youth is killed,
In halls where every fear is drilled.

The family time, a distant gleam,
In memories where the shadows seem,
A faded echo, a lost dream,
In pathways where the heart's esteem.

The elders in their twilight years,
Abandoned where the silence sears,
In old age homes where no one hears,
The tales of love, the whispered tears.

Progress, a path where hearts do strain,
In battles where the spirits wane,
The cost of dreams, a silent pain,
In shadows where the hopes remain.

Countries on the edge of war,
In conflicts where the shadows spar,
The cost of progress reaching far,
In fields where every soul's ajar.

Mental peace, a distant shore,
In races where the spirits bore,
The heart in shadows evermore,
In spaces where the dreams implore.

The world, in chaos, dreams of light,
In battles where the shadows fight,
The cost of progress in the night,
A silence where the truths ignite.

So let us pause, in silent grace,
To find the peace in every place,
To cherish love in every space,
In moments where the hearts embrace.

The Echoes of Our Love

In a small town where the river bends,
Where fields of jasmine never end,
A young love blossomed, fresh and pure,
Between a girl and boy demure.

Her hair, like silk in moonlit streams,
Her eyes, the heart of midnight dreams,
With laughter like a temple chime,
She danced through life in perfect rhyme.

He, with a spirit bold and kind,
A poet's heart and a thoughtful mind,
With eyes that held the morning sun,
In his embrace, her world was spun.

They met beneath a banyan tree,
Where prayers were whispered secretly,
In stolen glances, smiles so bright,
They shared their dreams in soft twilight.

The village spoke of their pure love,
A blessing from the stars above,
Their hearts entwined, a perfect blend,
Two souls as one, no need to pretend.

But fate is cruel, with unseen turns,
And love can blaze, then leave but burns.
A rift, a tear, in fragile thread,
Left words unsaid, hearts left unfed.

One evening, under skies of grey,
A shadow fell where light held sway,
Her father spoke of future plans,
A distant match, with stranger's hands.

Her eyes, once filled with joy and light,
Now clouded with a sorrowed night,
The boy, a dream now out of reach,
A silent cry, no words could breach.

He, broken-hearted, wandered far,
In night's embrace, a fallen star,
His poems turned to tears of ink,
In silence, on the brink.

The village murmured, hearts in pain,
In every drop of monsoon rain,
Two lovers torn by duty's call,
A cruel fate in shadows' thrall.

She, in her new home, never found
The echoes of their love's sweet sound,
With every breath, with every sigh,
She missed the love that passed her by.

He, in the fields of yellow gold,
Felt the weight of stories old,
A love that slipped through fingers thin,
A heart left bare, a soul within.

In temples where the incense burned,
In prayers where the heart returned,
The echoes of their love remained,
A tale of loss in memories chained.

The banyan tree, a silent sage,
Watched over every tear and page,
Where once they carved their names so true,
Now whispers of the past withdrew.

The beauty of a love so bright,
Now lost to fate's unyielding night,
A tragedy of hearts so young,
A song unsung, a life unstrung.

In every heart that feels their pain,
In every tear, in every rain,
Their story lives, a timeless lore,
Of love that lives forevermore.

A Love Unspoken

In fields of childhood's golden hue,
Where morning's light was fresh and new,
A boy and girl, with dreams so pure,
Shared laughter that could always cure.

She, with eyes like a monsoon rain,
And laughter like a sweet refrain,
He, with a heart that soared like wings,
In her presence, joy it brings.

Through schoolyard games and secret notes,
They wove a bond with tender quotes,
In silent glances, smiles bright,
Their hearts were joined in youthful light.

But life, with currents strong and wild,
Separated girl and boy, now exiled,
He to a school where boys would grow,
She where only girls would go.

Years rolled on in separate streams,
Their childhood faded into dreams,
Yet destiny had plans unseen,
To reunite them, crisp and clean.

In college halls, they met once more,
Where dreams of future filled the floor,
His heart still beat that youthful tune,
For her, beneath the same old moon.

But silence held his love so tight,
Though she, too, glowed in his sight,
His friend, a brother close and true,
Also loved her, but never knew.

Their days in class were bright with hope,
In shadows where their hearts would cope,
A dance of fate in every glance,
A love unspoken, no chance.

His friend, in silence, felt the flame,
Of love for her, without a name,
The boy, for friendship's sake, withdrew,
Though his heart whispered, "She loves you."

She, in secret, held her breath,
When near him, she was lost to death,
Her heart would race, her cheeks would flush,
In every silent, tender rush.

She felt the warmth of his desire,
A silent longing like a fire,
Yet words unsaid left hearts apart,
Though love had blossomed in her heart.

Graduation came, their paths aligned,
In every look, their love confined,
Yet courage failed, their hearts held back,
In fear of breaking friendship's track.

Then came a man, so bold and sure,
With courage that could love secure,
He asked her hand, she did not wait,
And life moved on with fleeting fate.

She married him, an unknown fate,
While he, in silence, mourned too late,
A love that slipped through fingers cold,
A story left to hearts untold.

In moments where their paths would cross,
He saw her smile, he felt the loss,
Yet in his heart, a warmth remained,
For love once shared, still unclaimed.

Her eyes would seek him now and then,
In shadows where the dreams begin,
She wondered what their love could be,
If he had spoken, set it free.

In fields of youth, where love was bright,
A bond of hearts in silent flight,
Their love, a tale of might-have-been,
A story of what lay within.

So let this tale of love inspire,
To speak the heart, to dare the fire,
For life is brief and love so true,
Deserves a voice to see it through.

Elegy for a Friend

In shadows where the memories fall,
Where echoes of your laughter call,
I stand alone, where grief stands tall,
In mourning where the shadows sprawl.

Your voice, a whisper on the breeze,
In echoes where the heartstrings seize,
A fleeting touch in whispered trees,
In moments where the spirit grieves.

We walked through days of golden light,
Through morning's grace, through evening's
flight,
In every step, in every sight,
A friendship where the heart's delight.

But now the world feels strangely cold,
In spaces where the silence's bold,
The stories left forever told,
In shadows where the grief's unrolled.

I see your smile in every dawn,
In every sunset, you are drawn,
A shadow where your spirit's gone,
In pathways where the heart's withdrawn.

The times we shared in laughter’s grace,
In every smile, in every face,
Are etched in memories’ soft embrace,
In whispers where the dreams retrace.

Your spirit now, a star's own light,
In heaven’s vast and silent night,
A beacon through the darkest flight,
A guide where every heart’s in sight.

I hold the moments we have known,
In spaces where our love has grown,
A seed where every dream was sown,
In echoes where the heart’s alone.

The pain of loss, a shadowed grief,
In every breath, in every leaf,
Reflects the silence, the disbelief,
In spaces where the tears are brief.

But in the night where silence falls,
Where shadows trace the hallowed halls,
I hear your voice in whispers’ calls,
In memories where the heart enthralls.

So let your spirit softly rest,
In heaven’s light, in peace’s quest,
A star where every heart’s confessed,
In dreams where love’s forever blessed.

In life's own dance, in love's own song,
Through every path, where hearts belong,
Your memory, in silence strong,
Will guide me where the nights are long.

The Unsung Builders

In far-flung lands where shadows sweep,
Where mountains rise and rivers leap,
They labor through the nights so deep,
The unsung builders, dreams they keep.

With hands that carve the earth and stone,
In valleys where the wind has grown,
They stand where progress is unknown,
In spaces where the heart's alone.

The roads they lay, the bridges strong,
In lands where ancient trees belong,
Their toil becomes the silent song,
In echoes where the hearts prolong.

In forests where the rivers flow,
In deserts where the hot winds blow,
They work through highs, they work through lows,
In fields where silent shadows grow.

Far from the comforts, far from ease,
In places where the spirits seize,
They build where only few would please,
In silence where the heart's appease.

No headlines tell of their great deeds,
In spaces where the spirit feeds,
They sow the seeds where future leads,
In pathways where the heart's accedes.

Their families wait in distant lands,
In homes where love and life expands,
While they shape dreams with calloused hands,
In fields where only silence stands.

The nation's strength in every mile,
In every bridge, in every aisle,
Is born from sweat where hearts compile,
In places where the shadows smile.

So let us honor, let us raise,
A song for those who build the ways,
On silent nights, on brightest days,
In pathways where their spirit stays.

For every road, for every span,
For every dream where progress ran,
We owe a debt to every man,
Who builds the world with silent plan.

The Pioneers of Science

In labs where silence sings the night,
Where minds ignite the darkest light,
The scientists, in quest of sight,
Forge paths through shadows, visions bright.

With atoms split and rockets soar,
Through space where dreams and futures bore,
They chart the stars and find the core,
In realms where spirits dare explore.

From medicine where life extends,
To codes where human knowledge blends,
They push the limits, find the ends,
In places where the future bends.

The moon and Mars, within their reach,
The distant stars, the silent speech,
In every test, in every breach,
A world where minds and hearts beseech.

The power born in atoms' dance,
In energies where dreams advance,
Reflects a world where every chance,
Is forged within the scientists' glance.

Through challenges where shadows creep,
Through nights where restless spirits sleep,
They hold the dreams, they sow the deep,
In spaces where the futures leap.

Names may shine in history's line,
In stories where the stars align,
But in the lab where spirits pine,
They work in silence, hearts benign.

For every cure, for every flight,
For every glimpse of future's light,
They walk through shadows, brave the night,
In places where the spirits fight.

So let us honor those who dream,
Who push the limits, light the beam,
In silent labs where futures teem,
With hopes where human hearts redeem.

In science where the spirits roam,
In visions where the hearts call home,
They build the paths where dreams will comb,
In shadows where the spirits loom.

The Greed of the Powerful

In halls where power's whispers twine,
Where promises like shadows line,
The powerful's greed defines,
A tale where hearts and dreams combine.
The oratory, once a grace,
Now lost in greed's unyielding chase,
Reflects a world where truths erase,
In shadows where the heart's debase.

They speak of hope, of dreams, of light,
In rhetoric where shadows fight,
But in the dark, beyond the sight,
They twist the truths where spirits bite.

The greed that fuels their silent plans,
In coffers where the power stands,
Corrupts the land where freedom's bans,
Are broken by their shadowed hands.

The people lost in chaos' snare,
In places where the shadows glare,
Find hope in words that do not care,
In echoes where the hearts despair.

The speeches filled with hollow might,
Where promises are lost from sight,

Reflect a world in endless night,
In places where the heart's contrite.

The degradation, swift and pure,
In words where only greed's allure,
Leaves hopes in silence, hearts unsure,
In pathways where the dreams endure.

Yet in the shadows, truth remains,
In whispers where the heart refrains,
A light that breaks the endless chains,
In spaces where the courage gains.

So let us see through shadows' veil,
Through words where only lies prevail,
To find the truth where hearts can sail,
In spaces where the spirits trail.

For in the end, the light will shine,
Through shadows where the hearts align,
And truth will break the silent line,
In places where the dreams consign.

9 789363 314269

Printed by Libri Plureos GmbH in Hamburg, Germany